Shift Happens

by Karen White

Masterpiece Press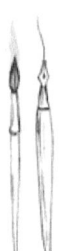

© 2020 by Karen White

All rights reserved. No part of this book may be used or reproduced in any manner whatsoever without written permission except in the case of brief quotations embedded in articles and reviews.

Magic of Memoir

It helps us to see and feel
Things that we never knew
We were looking for
But are so grateful to have found.
— Michelle Beckman

Acknowledgments

I want to thank...

- Writers from the Memoir and Write Like a Pro groups for their honest feedback and friendship
- Jean Reynolds for all her encouragement and technical support to help make this book possible
- My many friends for their encouragement and interest

Table of Contents

PART ONE **NOT FOR LACK OF TRYING**	1
Sharing My Story	3
Blaming the River	5
Music to My Ears	7
Star Reporter	9
High School Hustle	11
No Pain, No Gain	13
The Search	15
Challenged in Switzerland	17
Patience Is a Virtue	20
PART TWO **IN MY OPINION**	23
Pie: The Comfort Food	25
Connecting with the Stars	27
A Day in the Studio (Florida)	30
Solitude	34
Television Tempest 2018	36
I Miss Her Voice	39
Keeping up Appearances	42
Paris 1991	44
I'm Older than I've Ever Been	47

PART THREE	49
OH, YES I DID	
Going Under with a Hat	51
Unleash the Power?	53
Foolhardy or Fearless	56
Rocky Mountain High	60
Solo Show	63
Overcoming Indecision	65
A Little Chocolate Now and Then	68
Celebration of Life	70
PART FOUR	73
WHO COULD HAVE KNOWN	
Draw Me	77
Field Trip Fervor	80
Cross Signals	82
Denver, Colorado	84
Crack in the Night	86
Art Studio	89
California Dreamin'	92
Ah, Wilderness!	94
Death Valley Days	98
Connecting the Dots	101
The Purge	103

PART FIVE	107
TAKING A STAND	
Finding My Moral Compass in the 60s	109
Road Not Taken	111
The Shrine Project	114
Shift Happens	119
Hope Is Exhausting	121
And Yet We Persist	125
ABOUT THE AUTHOR	128

PART ONE

NOT FOR LACK OF TRYING

Sharing My Story

If I ever had a favorite place to hang out, it would be the Tattered Cover Bookstore. In Denver we had the biggest, best bookstore in the West—designed with a reading nook in every corner, a coffee shop and overstuffed chairs. The space was bright with large windows, the bookshelves wove in and out of every room of the four-story building. It was an inspiration to readers and writers.

I spent evenings and some Sunday afternoons browsing. I always left with an assortment of magazines, mysteries, biographies and art books.

Even though I appreciated good writing. I never thought then about crafting a story of my own. I felt I couldn't put a string of sentences together for a coherent composition.

But strange things happened when I left Denver—I started to write. Well, that's what I called it. I hadn't found my voice yet, so my pieces were an amalgam of my favorite authors, some writing-tool suggestions and too many metaphors. Most of those essays just seemed tedious and meaningless.

I eventually decided to join a writing group so I could see how others approached the subject. It's not that my life is that interesting, but I wanted to understand it better.

I showed up every session to participate. I was uncertain at first about reading my work out loud. I felt shy and then confident and then disappointed and then exhilarated, and those feelings never went away. But they lessened in intensity as I gained confidence in what I have to say and how I say it. As an artist I also know failure can be that moment when the creative process blooms.

In writing a personal essay:

I learned to tell the truth—my truth, not another's. I learned to pick one subject and stay with it. (I once read that a personal essay can be reduced to one word.) I learned just because it happened to me does not make it interesting. And I learned to show up and share.

Some of my colleagues express their lives through poetry, family life stories and risky past confessions. We have shared our memories of common experiences like divorce, deaths, ringer washers, Saturday matinees, milk delivery and white Wonder Bread sandwiches. We've got something to say, and we've said it the best we could.

So little by little and story by story, I have a notebook full of essays. I view my memoirs as getting a second chance at my life with a little revelation. Who knows, someday my book might be on the shelf of the Tattered Cover Bookstore.

Blaming the River

I struggled to stay afloat in the muddy river. My father's idea of teaching me how to swim was to throw me out of the boat. I hit the water. I didn't swim. I panicked, took in water and went under. My brother, a child himself, jumped in and pulled me out.

In the summer, we shared a cottage with another family by the Walhonding River. My brothers and I were free to go in the water whenever we wanted. They could swim. Inner tubes and a rowboat were at our disposal. We navigated to our little island full of willows, mudflats and sand in a leaky boat, fighting the current to stay on course.

In spite of my sink-or-swim episode, I continued playing in the water—although timidly and only up to my knees. Large rocks and unexpected holes in the river bottom prevented me from wading far from shore. I never learned to swim. I played on the island in my mud-caked Keds. The area smelled of decaying fish, warm summer air, algae and wet clay. In the hot sun I built little sculptures with stones, twigs, fish bones and feathers while my brothers caught tadpoles and frogs. I routinely sunburned until my skin hesitantly tanned.

I felt conflicted most of the time there. Even as I tried to convince myself that I enjoyed the river—I waited anxiously for the summer to pass. A stubborn preference for my paper dolls and story books occupied my mind, but still I looked for washed-up stones that felt smooth and hot in my fingers. We always used the smooth, flat ones to skip across the water.

Those days the river seemed to glint more light than it should since the water always looked murky. We were upstream from the Paper Mill but downstream from another factory. The grownups fished for carp and catfish from the river bank a few feet from the cottage. You had to wonder about the fish.

At the end of the day, away from the river, I reveled in the sight of lightning bugs and earth worms that came out at night, but not the mosquitoes that fought for space on my skin amid poison ivy and sunburn blisters. The sound of baseball on the radio, the shuffle of a deck of cards and the light of kerosene lanterns filled the cottage on warm summer evenings.

Those months on the river were full. Our family returned for several years and I became a reluctant tomboy hanging out with my brothers. At times, I saw a dark, unfriendly river and other times it seemed a benign part of summer, part of Ohio, part of small town living in the 50's.

But still, every so often I blame the river for those summers.

Music to My Ears (Ohio 1948)

Music could have been a rich part of my life. I brooded over this while feeling the wind on top of Roscoe Hill. Seeing the red brick house brought back memories. Flower beds and trees of all kinds seemed to parade throughout the hilly landscape surrounding my mother's family home.

When I visited as a child, I played hopscotch on the slate walk and rolled down a sloped yard that had unusually soft fine grass. On those lazy summer days I whiled away afternoons on the front-porch swing reading and daydreaming. Melodies sifted through the screen door.

Inside, beyond the living room, past the dining room on the left, was the back room. It was a small space that housed a built-in hutch, the stairs to the second floor and a carved upright piano stacked with sheet music from Glass's Music Store. The smell of musty carpets and old wood lingered. Even so, this is where my grandparents made music that was magic to my ears.

Grandpa played the guitar and the harmonica. He was a colorful character with his steel-stringed Depression era guitar and his Royal Concerto mouth harp. Grandma, more solemn, played the piano and sang gospel tunes and popular songs of the times. "You are My Sunshine" was her favorite.

Longing to learn how to make music, I pestered them constantly. But I grew disappointed because my grandparents were reluctant to teach any of their instruments. So, as a youngster, I sat at the piano striking the keys and looking at the sheet-music trying to make sense of it. I blew into the harmonica; I strummed the guitar yearning for my efforts to sound melodic. I wasn't a child prodigy.

    Yet, I never knew what their reticence was about. I only know that their music died with them in that red brick house on Roscoe Hill.

Star Reporter

She was dazzling. Each illustrated Brenda Starr strip twinkled with tiny stars. I tried to imagine what it was like to be self-assured, successful Brenda with her incredible good looks, sparkling eyes and long red hair. I got my kid scissors and cut out the comics.

One day around my eighth birthday I was lying on the floor reading Little Lulu, Prince Valiant and Pogo in the Sunday funny papers. I came across a comic strip called BRENDA STARR, REPORTER.

She was the "star" reporter on a fictional newspaper called THE FLASH; she always got the story. What a powerful message for a young girl in the 50's: an entire comic strip centered around an ambitious, adventurous female reporter. I pasted her picture in my school notebook.

At that time I needed inspiration, and she was it. I had just signed up for a speech contest at school but started to regret it right away. I was shy yet venturesome. Those conflicting characteristics always got me into trouble. My classmate Timmy, the favorite to win, usually won class competitions with his winning smile and confident attitude.

Nevertheless, I wrote my speech on 3 x 5 index cards to practice. I wanted to be good at this. I wanted to win, to be precise, just like the Star Reporter who got the story. Sometimes, I would stand in front of the mirror picturing myself with stars in my hair, dazzling the audience. Mostly, though, I fretted. Still, rehearsing daily, my confidence grew.

Eventually, the contest day arrived. The school basement was set up with rows of chairs, with a table of homemade goodies toward the back by the piano. Parents and school kids arrived, filling the seats. I wore my best dress, a yellow one my mother made.

Timmy gave his speech first. He looked self-assured in his white shirt and tie, smiling like he knew he had won. My turn came after several others. I stood behind the podium clutching my index cards, my hands shaking. I started out slowly but finished courageously. I knew I had this.

Finally, the teachers and parents voted. It was unanimous. I won!

I don't remember anything about the prize, but I fantasized that our local newspaper would print the winner's name in the Sunday paper the same day Brenda Starr, Star Reporter appeared in the funny papers in full color.

High School Hustle

Think left and think right and think low and think high. Oh, the thinks you can think up if only you try. - Dr. Seuss

I would rather have done anything than to be in high school. What I remember is that I was searching for meaning, trying to fit in and looking for a creative outlet—basically, having an existential crisis at fifteen.

Despite teenage angst, hormones and ambivalence I was inquisitive and eager to learn. Much of my energy centered on being a good student because I planned on becoming the first in my family to go to college. I graduated second in my class and obtained a college scholarship.

I didn't think too much about a profession (how to make money) in high school—we didn't have vocational day during freshman year to encourage us to plan our future. Our school had very few resources. An art curriculum did not exist at Sacred Heart High, so the nuns, aware of my talent from grade school, insisted I craft all the holiday decorations and produce the prom designs. In that context, I enjoyed artist status among my peers.

The bigger picture was this: I had hoped to paint, draw, play the piano, stage a play, learn various art forms or discover renowned artists and enjoy museums with a contemporary collection, but the school had nothing to offer. Therefore, the speed with which I could get out of high school seemed paramount.

Acting out my frustrations landed me in the principal's office a few times. It was strange.

I should probably mention that for a while I considered being a reporter because of comic-book legend Brenda Starr, star reporter for THE FLASH. But the school didn't have a creative writing class either, and I was pretty sure I needed some instruction. I stuck with the talent I knew I had.

With hindsight, I can see that rock n' roll was the adolescent salvation of the time, and we could dance until our knee socks slouched. I can see that we girls were well dressed, with poodle skirts, saddle shoes and circle pins. I can see that Nancy Drew and her cadre of teen mystery writers entertained us. It wasn't all bad.

Still I couldn't wait to graduate and leave town for college—a place where I might be able to become the only thing I wanted to become, an artist.

No Pain, No Gain

I always wanted to be somebody, but now I see I should have been more specific. —Lily Tomlin

I was a sight to behold, outfitted in an oversized crepe dress with a fox stole, wobbling in my mother's high heels, a candy cigarette dangling from my lips. I had a large box of dress-up clothes—an assortment of adult textile-rationed old dresses along with shoes, purses, jewelry and hats. My made-up life of the 40s and 50s extended to a substantial paper-doll collection bought from the five and dime. Each movie star had a glamorous assortment of gowns, suits and swimwear—many I designed myself.

These inventive play times must have prepared me for a creative life.

The moment I arrived in Columbus, in the 1960s, I began building a life around school, art, work and new friends. During my time in the Art Department at Ohio State University (OSU), my studio courses included printmaking, ceramics, figurative and abstract sculpture, modern painting, drawing, photography and art history. A dream come true.

At that time the prevailing art form in the U.S. was Abstract Expressionism—nonrepresentational painting. Men dominated the art scene all around the country, and women artists working to establish their careers were usually eclipsed.

The path ahead of me appeared challenging. Nevertheless, immersed in a culture of art in one of the biggest art departments in the state, and with the desire and ambition to be an artist, I took advantage of the environment. I liked it there, liked the smell of paint and clay, the big windows in each studio and the anticipation of each new class. I liked the creative process but struggled to find my voice in abstract painting and began looking for more inspiration.

This new inspiration came with the feminist art movement of the late 60s and 70s. Female artists began to influence and establish art in women's experiences and values, which meant that figurative imagery, portraiture and decorative arts opened up new avenues for everyone.

Women artists now insisted on a balance of representation in art centers and museums by actively protesting for equity in those exhibits. This movement had a big influence on me, I abandoned the traditional art department curriculum and tackled the techniques of fiber arts and collage. These styles were slow to be recognized by the art establishment. Still, I carried on.

I had a flair for sculptural and dimensional concepts and my newly designed fiber sculptures won several awards in the state, thereby securing my first art exhibit in a gallery next to campus. I was in my 20s.

I'd felt since I was a child that I would have art in my life, and I'm glad I was right.

The Search

My mother died at age 52. I had gone home for the funeral and had the task to sort through her personal effects and dispose of them. I willingly did this hoping I could learn something new about who she was. I never felt she revealed much of herself.

The last time I visited they were building their dream home, a ranch style outside of town in a meadow with a stream and a few trees—she and her second husband. I didn't move through the house claiming anything of my mother's —I went to her room where her personal possessions were.

The closet door was slightly open—it seemed to be an invitation to start there. I couldn't imagine what I might find behind the clothes or in the boxes on the shelves. The hanging rod full of blouses, dresses and slacks looked old and out of style. I bagged them for the thrift store. The casual clothes reflected what she liked: to go fishing and work in the yard. I remember she loved the smell of roses and lilacs, those things nourished her. She also liked cocktails and cigarettes—those things destroyed her.

I ignored the shoes lining the closet floor: boots, Keds and flats. My attention flew to the top shelf, where I saw a camera and some unidentified boxes. I carefully placed them on the floor to rummage through, but I found no secret life hidden in unmarked cartons.

I moved on to the chest-of-drawers and vanity, done in a light wood veneer; they seemed most likely to conceal a mystery. I carefully pulled her belongings from the drawers and sorted through them one by one, watchful not to miss anything. And then, there in the bottom of a drawer, rested a discolored envelope with softly worn edges. No name on the front.

I sat on the bed and anxiously opened the envelope addressed to no one. I could hear the TV in the other room, wind blowing outside and someone cooking in the kitchen. The letter—brown with age—had been carefully concealed for years. I was at first puzzled by who wrote it and who it was intended for, and then I got the picture. My maternal grandmother had written the note to my father when he married my mother, admonishing him to be a good and caring husband to her precious daughter. It was a somewhat bitter and yet heartfelt poem that my mother had kept to herself all these years.

I pocketed the letter, knowing this was the only secret I was going to find.

And what was there for me to see? Nothing but a few boxes adding up to a lifetime. No travel mementos, no journal, no last letter to her children and no indication of what her dreams might have been. She would see it as a kind of pride—not leaving a lot of stuff behind. But, for me, I looked for something she was not willing to share. I wanted to believe my mother had dreams, unrealized or not: still I wanted to know.

Challenged in Switzerland

Looking back, the youth hostel seemed like a really bad idea. I traveled to Basel, Switzerland in 1991 to show my art and to attend an international art workshop. It was my first time showing in Europe, and I wanted to make a good impression and have a good time. I was off to a bad start.

After arriving on the bullet train from Paris, I took a tram to my destination—a youth hostel. A group from the States and European countries associated with the workshop reserved the hostel for a week. The youth hostel, a large, centuries-old three-story stone building, stood regally in a cluster of trees in old town Basel. It looked inviting.

Weary from traveling and very little sleep, I was surprised early the next morning when the hostel folks ushered everyone out and locked the doors for the rest of the day —even though the town bicentennial had kept everyone up all night with fireworks. We were annoyed, but we headed toward a cafe.

With caffeine in hand, I walked to the Kunstmuseum determined to make the best of my day. An impressive place, the museum displayed the Old Masters, as well as contemporary paintings and sculpture. Amid the art I saw a cluster of chairs and a sofa. I sat down. I don't know how long I had been asleep before someone was shaking me. The museum closed at noon on Saturday, they said. I had to leave. Again.

Outside, rain had started to fall. I roamed around the city streets almost frantic with the weariness and loneliness you can only experience in a foreign country. My fellow travelers had left for a side trip.

Still, I decided to see the city before returning to the boarding house. I saw a few historic sites and a postcard view of the Rhine River, and then I met the international artists for gallery night. We rode the tram and taxis around town to all the art shows, finally arriving at the gallery where my art was exhibited. Unfortunately, after we got lost a few times during the late evening, the gallery was closed when we got there. Disappointment was palpable. I had traveled halfway around the world and missed my own show.

The next morning someone handed me a newspaper. The local art column had reviewed a select group of shows and artists. I was one of them—I could see my name in print, but I couldn't read German. Did I really want to know what it said? Eventually, though, I got a few sentences translated from the newspaper feature: "Among the most interesting pieces belong to American artist Karen White." They continued, "In these pieces White poses questions about the scope of sculpture. American White is not only more advanced in public resonance than her European colleagues but also in poetic presentation. In total, 75 artists from the USA, Canada, Israel, South

America, Europe, Taiwan and Japan are showing their work here."

The previous day's letdown seemed bearable now. An appreciative art review in the newspaper can work miracles.

At the airport, on my way back to the States, I learned my flight had been canceled. I waited in the terminal, tolerating another sleepless night, but a smile pulled at me as I was comforted by the local newspaper tucked under my arm.

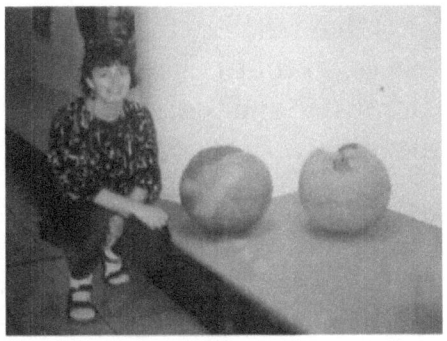

Patience Is a Virtue: How a Rubber Tree and a Renovation Taught Me Endurance

"Instant gratification takes too long," said Carrie Fisher, and I have to agree. I can be impatient, anxious, not reckless, but intolerant of plodding.

When I first moved to a rental on 14th Street in the Denver Capitol Hill area, around the corner in our alley was a florist supplier. I noticed they tossed plants that failed to thrive or didn't get sold during the week. I routinely plucked those plants from the dumpster and took them home to be revived. Amid some drooping brown leaves, I saw slim green shoots and felt hope.

The supplier threw out Boston ferns, heartleaf philodendron, spider plants, English ivy, ficus and a rubber tree. In a short amount of time, with careful tending, I had an actual forest of greenery in our temporary house.

That floriculture experience happened at a good time because I needed to see progress in something while taking on a bigger project.

My partner and I had bought a rundown turn-of-the-century brick commercial building, in downtown Denver, with the idea of transforming it into an artist studio and loft space. We showed up for hard work, day and night for months that turned into years. I experienced frustration, long hours and very little visible progress before we could see any transformation.

I wanted the strenuous work to be over and to enjoy my bright airy studio space. I struggled and gave up hope many times, whereas my partner got lost in the process and seemed to enjoy the slow rebuilding of a fossil.

The houseplants, on the other hand, responded almost immediately to me and fresh soil, bigger pots, water and sunlight.

Yet the building didn't blossom. It seemed at times there was never enough money, time or energy to resurrect that stubborn old structure. But we carried on.

Then one day I could see we were making progress. Eventually, with a mix of exasperation and expectation, we restored that brick building to a showcase that was featured in the newspapers.

We moved in with our forest of plants. The ficus expanded to a 13-foot tree growing up into our clerestory skylight. The rubber tree grew to 10 feet in a bank of west windows.

Yes, the building finally blossomed one spring, along with the plants, but I'll always remember that the journey took way too long.

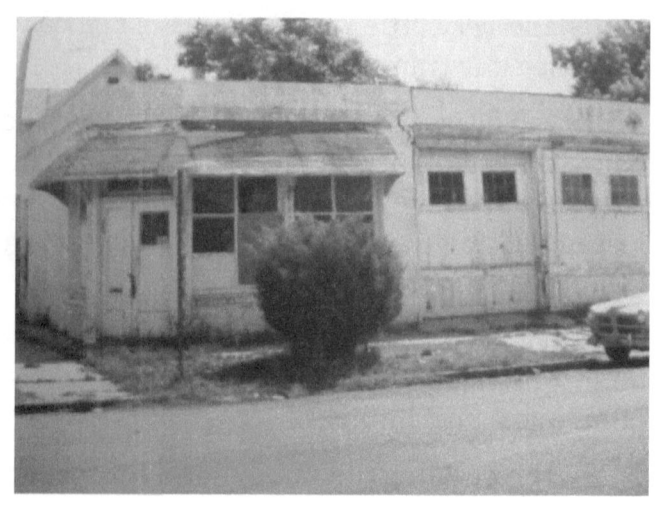

PART TWO

IN MY OPINION

Pie: The Comfort Food

We must have pie. Stress cannot exist in the presence of a pie.—David Mamet

I like pie: cherry pie, apple pie, pumpkin pie, peach pie and cream pie.

Pie comforted me as a child, made me smile and gave me something to look forward to. I ate a lot of pie. My mother made those oven fresh, sweet-smelling treats from our bounty of fruit trees in the backyard. We had three apple trees, two cherry trees, one peach tree, a grape arbor and a pear tree. Sometimes the neighbor would share her raspberry patch, although I regularly helped myself. Spring brought about a batch of rhubarb and a row of strawberries in the garden. I didn't know how fortunate I was.

I remember going for rides with my grandparents, in their 1950 green Plymouth, to Amish country for fresh pie. I usually got car sick riding in the back seat. Yet, this is what we did on Sunday afternoons—drive those curvy, hilly Ohio back roads. One of those Sundays I got my finger slammed in the car door. I recall to this day how badly that hurt. Still, throughout the many discomforts was the anticipation of Amish fruit pies just ahead. I hoped for a slice of fresh baked peach—the kind with the crisscross crust on top.

One of my favorite movies - with a pie scene - is *Michael,* featuring John Travolta as the amorous archangel and Andie MacDowell as a self-proclaimed angel expert. I loved the particular segment in a shabby diner where the group ordered homemade pies—one of every kind. The angel expert, an erstwhile poet and songwriter, wrote a poem that started and ended with:

Pie, pie,

Me oh my

I love pie.

I've seen that movie a few too many times.

Occasionally I would visit the House of Pies on Colorado Boulevard in Denver for a piece of mocha-almond-fudge-delight.

I'm not much of a cook or baker, but I managed to make pies through the years. Peach-rhubarb was a specialty and later pumpkin pie with plant milk and maple syrup. A whole-wheat crust was a breeze with a Cuisinart.

I don't make fruit pies anymore. Now I buy them at the grocery and try not to eat the whole thing in one sitting. Yogi Berra once said—and I agree—"Cut my pie into four pieces: I don't think I could eat eight."

Connecting with the Stars

Recently, I watched a segment of the *New Yorker Magazine* TV series about a group of people who had witnessed several funny incidents with Bill Murray. He's the legendary guy in the movie *Groundhog Day* and TV's *Saturday Night Live*.

The viewing audience caught a glimpse of the personalities of the group as they sat in a circle drinking coffee in a church basement on alternate Saturdays between twelve-step programs and rummage sales. This Bill Murray bunch took the time to share a hilarious story about an encounter each had with the actor in New York City. I had to wonder why that was so important to them. Do we transcend our lives by connecting with bigger lives?

Several times throughout my life I've nearly connected with a "bigger life." The earliest recollection: I was in middle school and a rock n' roll Band featuring pop stars came through town. I couldn't sleep for a week thinking about it.

The band was scheduled to play at the county fairgrounds. The place smelled like wet cattle and soggy straw - definitely not the Troubadour in Los Angeles. When the tour bus arrived, I was in the crowd with the rest of the townies to watch the teen idols step out of the bus into the Performance Hall. The older girls boasted of having backstage passes and were able to parlay their brush-with-celebrity into being more popular for an entire year. I took note of that.

My opportunity came later in life when I had a few drinks with John Denver during the time he lived in Aspen in the 80s. I shook hands with Gloria Steinem during a round table discussion in Colorado. I definitely felt like I had connected with a bigger life.

Lately, I learned Ernest Hemingway stayed at my condo, back then a hotel, and sunned himself on my porch. This was around 1943. I had no direct contact with him, but I'm willing to live a bigger life by association.

I haven't been able to find out why he stayed at the Haven Hotel; perhaps a function at Cypress Gardens, suggested a friend. Esther Williams stayed at the hotel too while filming *Easy to Love*, and Calvin Coolidge had his photo taken on my front steps. I already feel like a better person knowing this. Also I'm inspired to write knowing Hemingway sipped his whiskey in the old rocker, imagining a new novel, on that porch—now my studio.

I don't pretend to write like Hemingway, though on a good day I can put together a pretty good essay. I don't have answers to why people feel it's important to acknowledge celebrity. Yet, we tap into our fantasies whether in a church basement, the county fair or the Haven porch. I'm happy to transcend my everyday life, occasionally, for a larger one by connecting with the stars.

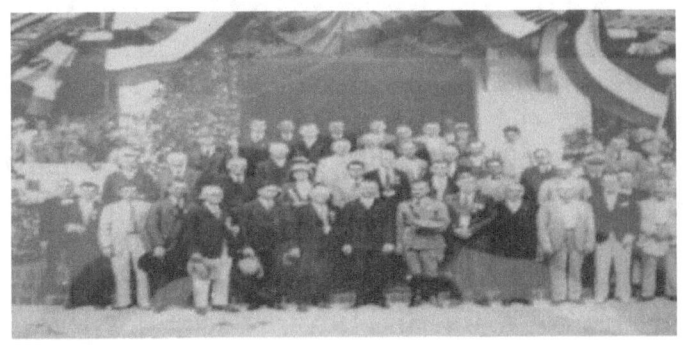

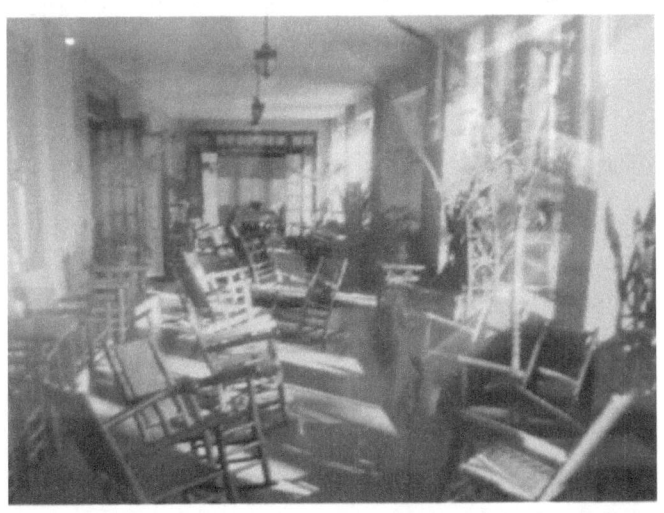

A Day in the Studio (Florida)

I always want a successful day in the studio, like an obsession, but I don't always get it. My studio time is about solving a creative problem. I usually design a piece around a story I want to tell, although the narrative might not be evident to the viewer. I've always resisted a "realism" approach to art: I use form, line and texture to communicate.

Telling a story necessitates adhering to the aesthetic principles and the elements of design, and that sometimes feels like a skirmish at the drawing board. How can I tell this story and achieve a sense of balance with a satisfying composition? Age-old questions.

My studio is a large, sunny room in my condo—because of recent downsizing, it's one of the smallest workspaces I've had. I've combined work and living space for most of my creative life. One location, big or small, works best for me.

I can open a window and hear the birds sing in the palm trees. I'm a morning worker, and I wait for the dawn to break so natural light can fill my studio. I never work after dark.

The art process sometimes feels like a puzzle—jostling pieces and shapes and textures until it resonates. I often work on several pieces at once. Gradually, a piece starts to reveal itself to me despite my occasional wrestling with the materials. When the art comes together, I have a sensation of gliding and I feel courageous with every selection I make.

Other days when I'm struggling, I wonder why I ever became an artist. But that's the amazing, irritating, joyful, desperate, terrifying, stimulating thing about creating—the process is a conundrum.

Toward the end of the day, I put the materials away in the proper drawers, shelves, or boxes. I sweep the red tile floor and tidy up so I can have a fresh space for the next day.

It's really all I ever want to do, and I can't resist doing it all over again despite the enigma of being entirely devoted to my art and endlessly frustrated by it.

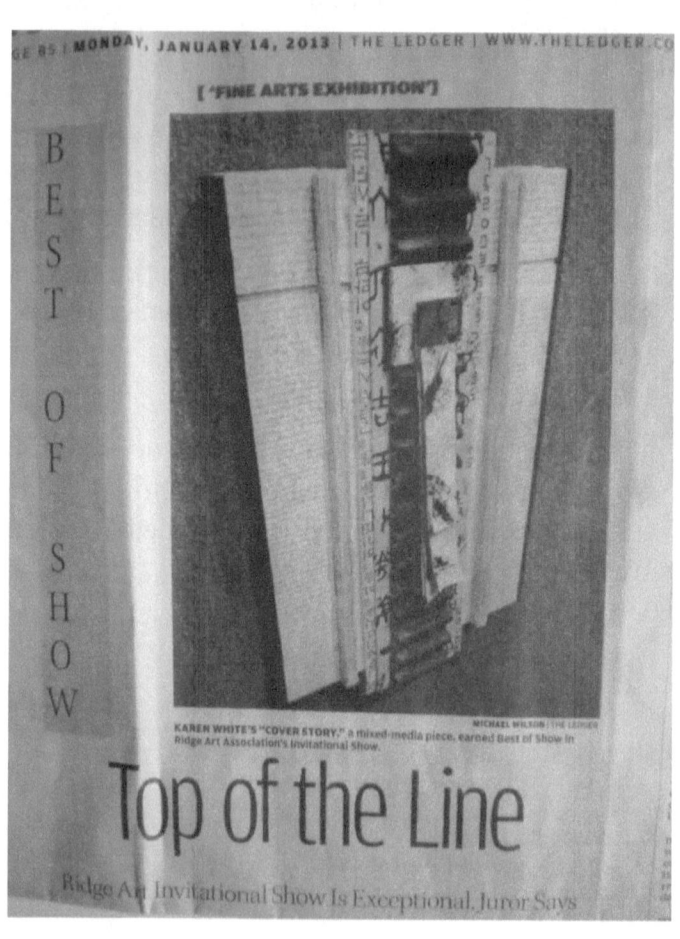

['REFLECTIONS']

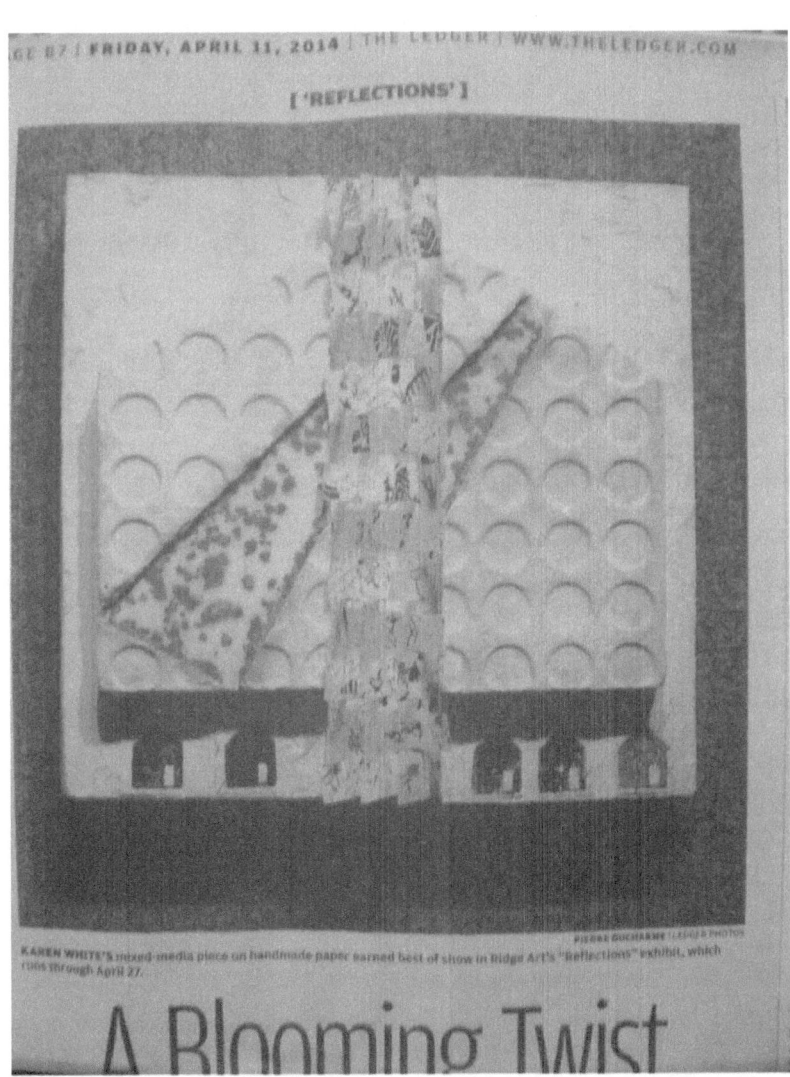

KAREN WHITE'S mixed-media piece on handmade paper earned best of show in Ridge Art's "Reflections" exhibit, which runs through April 27.

A Blooming Twist

Solitude

Solitude is delicious in the years of maturity. — Einstein

The heavy metal door had to be tugged open. Tall shelving wrapped around the main room of the Library like sentries. Wooden tables lined up, one after another, in the middle of each room and the heavy chairs, on marble floors, always skidded with a screech when I pulled one out—a surprising sound in that cavernous space.

That gray stone building dominated the corner of Fourth and Chestnut, one block from Main Street, in my hometown. It was designed to look imposing with large columns at the front entrance. Lettering on the door's glass insert read *Coshocton Public Library*.

I don't know where I got my love of reading. I don't remember being read bedtime stories. My family generally just read the newspaper, but my mom had a small bookcase with a few novels and a poetry book. She always said she didn't have time to sit and read.

But I sat and read. We had a large slightly worn chair that I could be found curled up in or my legs draped over the arm, my face buried in a book. I read Nancy Drew and Edgar Allan Poe. I read movie magazines and teen magazines. I read comic books and poetry. I read what interested me.

When I wasn't reading in my chair, I walked to the library—three blocks away. I got my first lending card there. It was a small card with the official seal of Ohio in green ink.

I remember my library as a place of solitude, and I felt somewhat secluded in the stacks. I liked feeling solitary amid the books. Author Anna Quindlen said, "Reading was for me then a way of lifting myself out of a crowded environment into a place where I could be by myself."

I can't help but contrast this picture with today's multi-purpose libraries. Currently the library is a rendezvous for after-school kids, a day care center for exuberant youngsters, a source of computers for the computerless, a day shelter for the homeless, a resource for the jobless, a hub to pick up inter-library books, a gathering place to see a movie, join a book club or take a class. All in all, an asset to the community. I admit I take advantage of some of those resources, and I also help the library set up even more programs for the general public.

Still, I want from time to time, to recharge in my old library with its quiet place to read and uninterrupted place to write. I agree with Henry David Thoreau who said, " I never found a companion that was so companionable as solitude."

I don't know, maybe being solitary is a lost art.

Television Tempest 2018

I spent Sunday evenings with my neighbors watching the *Ed Sullivan Show* when I was growing up. My family didn't get a TV until much later. And when we finally did, I watched that black and white, 13-inch screen all the time, captivated by a brand new world of advertisement and adventure. We relied on our roof-mounted all-directional antenna kit for spotty reception.

I liked to watch *Howdy Doody, Gunsmoke, Father Knows Best,* and *Your Hit Parade.* My teen years were anchored to *American Bandstand* and *The Jack Paar Show.* My parents watched the news—preoccupied with Khrushchev and Castro and the Cold War. We had become dependent on the screen.

But the old TVs didn't always work. Those large consoles were always on the fritz: either the picture rolled, the sound didn't work or the horizontal couldn't be controlled. The knobs, designed to correct those situations, only teased us. Frustrated, we fiddled with the rabbit ears until we were frantic.

Many times the vacuum tubes had to be removed to the nearest drugstore that had a self-service TV tube-tester. Eventually, the bad ones were replaced with new ones from the locked bottom drawer of the U-Test-M.

TV watching is so much more convenient and visually satisfying today. When my high-definition television acts up—I call the cable company who magically restores it over the phone, and another thing, I'm happy to have a remote. I have 300 channels instead of the merely three networks we all started out with.

I recently decided I don't need all those channels. I called the cable company and explained that I'd like a few essential channels at $29.99 as advertised. Right away I felt self-righteous knowing I would save $100 a month, but before I had a chance to feel too smug the representative told me this was not possible. She made clear that since I already had the premium package, I was not eligible for the cost-saving Basic plan.

Well, to paraphrase a recurring character on the early season of TV's *Saturday Night Live*, Roseanne Roseannadanna, "Just goes to show, it's always something —you either got an old TV that doesn't work or a new one that does, but a cable company that doesn't care."

So I dropped my premium package altogether and wired my television to an antenna. Yes, an antenna, the type of receiver I started out with 50 years ago. This update is not a jumble of pipes and wires on the roof, but a convenient wall-mount digital indoor antenna about the size of a cereal box. I'm happy with it. Like my parents, I apprehensively watch the news and fear the new cold war. All that's missing is a black-and-white TV set.

I Miss Her Voice

I saw author Nora Ephron as the voice of women everywhere struggling with the vicissitudes of life. She had our back. But she died a few years ago (2012).

Known for her quick wit, Nora was born to tell a story. She wrote essays, novels and plays. She was a New York resident, well known for her screenplays, particularly *When Harry Met Sally* and *You've Got Mail*. She was also appreciated for her celebrity-infused dinner parties. Everyone wanted to be around her. She was the woman friend we all wished for: witty, irreverent, confident and talented.

I remember seeing the movie *Heartburn* about her turbulent marriage to Watergate reporter Carl Bernstein. She wrote openly about his infidelity, and that text soon became a go-to book for women facing divorce. That was a few years before I faced divorce.

The first book of hers that I read was *Crazy Salad: Some Things about Women* published in 1975. It's a collection of essays about the women's movement. At that time I was learning about feminism. I attended those conscious-raising groups she delighted us with and the National Women's Political Caucus she introduced to the world.

Nora wrote for *Esquire* magazine trying to give men a picture of the new feminism. She was the first to admit she didn't have a clear picture at times of this new movement. I appreciated those stories, written with self-effacing humor and humility.

Her intimate humor became more entertaining as she grew older, especially when she wrote about the "tribulations of maintenance and menopause."

She published *I Feel Bad About My Neck* in 2006. I don't know any other author who could pull off a title like that. She maintains "we all look good for our age. Except for our neck." For example, she says, "you have to cut open a redwood tree to see how old it is, but you wouldn't have to if it had a neck."

In 2010 her final book—*I Remember Nothing*—is an amusing riff about the challenges of memory loss. She says, "On some level, my life has been wasted on me. After all, if I can't remember it, who can?" Well, I can remember her life, but I'm stumbling over recollections of my own; nevertheless, like her I'll keep a sense of humor about it.

One of my favorite passages about her aging body reads: "You're two inches shorter than you used to be. You're ten pounds fatter, and you cannot lose a pound of it to save your soul. Your hands don't work as well as they once did, and you can't open bottles, jars or wrappers. If you were stranded on a desert island and your food were sealed in a plastic package, you would starve."

For Nora there was only one way to deal with life, and that was through her wit with a touch of whimsy.

I miss Nora Ephron and all the punchlines she might have written about the complexities of the world we live in now. I miss her voice.

Keeping up Appearances

Loose-fitting clothes are coming back. I like baggy clothes—the Annie Hall look. It's a look made famous by Woody Allen in his 1977 movie *Annie Hall*. The star, Diane Keaton, made the style legendary by sporting baggy trousers and large shirts with a scarf or a tie.

Right now I can only say I dress comfortably, reflecting some of that Look. I was glancing through the *New York Times Style* magazine and noticed that nothing advertised was appropriate for older women. I can't see myself wearing combat boots with mesh stockings, as pictured, or going around with untied shoelaces—that's an accident waiting to happen at my age.

I'm not sure I care anymore about fashion this time of my life, and that's liberating.

When I was growing up, my mother made my clothes, and here's the thing about those homemade outfits: you could not be certain whether you looked foolish or stylish with clothes made from Simplicity sewing patterns.

I could tell, as a child, that my newly sewn clothes didn't fit very well—they were too big: the shoulders drooped, the waist sagged, and the hem was too long. My mother always said after she proudly finished a dress "Don't forget: this is going to shrink." Since she didn't prewash the fabric, she routinely made them bigger to allow for shrinkage. I guess that was my first Annie Hall look.

In the 50s I started shopping for my clothes at our local department stores like J. C. Penney and J. J. Newberry. The wood floors creaked, and the old buildings smelled musty despite the advertised new fashions. Those tight pencil skirts looked pretty good with my saddle shoes.

In college we wore multicolored peasant style clothes. I started to sew my clothes then—large floral skirts were popular and easy to make. Then the mini skirt arrived, and it took less time to sew and still less fabric.

Before I moved to Florida, I got rid of my outdated clothes. I had a closet full of jackets that I was sure someone could use —despite the shoulder pads. I tried giving them away. Author Anna Quindlen once said, "You cannot give those suits away. You have to drive a Silver Stake through their lapels." Point taken.

If I won a shopping trip to my favorite boutique today, I'm not sure what style I would select. I probably would buy more of the black, white and beige casual clothes that already fill my closet. Yet it's liberating not to care if I'm wearing the latest fashion, a certain brand or mismatched prints.

As long as it's roomy.

Paris 1991

We went to the moon before we put wheels on suitcases. —Sen Nag

I had a set of black canvas LL Bean luggage with shoulder straps that I lugged around France and Switzerland. That's what comes to mind when I think of Paris. It must have been the weight of the bags, the inconvenience, the lack of mobility that beset me. I always thought I would have had a better time without the baggage.

Arriving at Charles de Gaulle from an overnight Atlantic flight, I navigated the streets with my bags to find a cab to the 9th Arrondissement. Our hotel was a converted nunnery—a unique flavor of Paris. It was our wedding anniversary, and despite fatigue and a quarrelsome mood, we found a lovely Parisian cafe.

Paris can be a delight of the senses: the pleasure of French food and the smell of the boulangeries. I read in the *Smithsonian Magazine* that food is culture: it guides our travels and it offers the aesthetic pleasures of great art.

Leaving the luggage behind I saw the architecture of the city. I loved the monumental Gothic cathedrals like Notre-Dame and Sainte-Chapelle on the Île de la Cité and Chartres Cathedral in the nearby country. The concrete and stone statues and gargoyles astonished. I can see why Gothic architecture inspired Victor Hugo to write *The Hunchback of Notre Dame* featuring extraordinary steeples, spires and dark shadows. In contrast Sainte-Chapelle was full of color and light because of the large medieval stained-glass windows —like sitting in the midst of a magic lighthouse.

The next day I set off on my own to see the museums. I stepped from the underground Metro at the western edge of Paris during a sultry August. Up the flight of stairs through an ornate iron trellis was a grand entrance to an inspiring view. The enormous glass Pyramid rose from the center of the courtyard that was the focal point of the Louvre Museum. I stood before the world's greatest, most renowned museum of art as a tourist with a fanny pack and a money belt. *C'est magnifique.*

I attempted to see as much of the 35,000 *objets d'art* as I could. I saw Egyptian and Roman antiquities, monumental sculptures in newly created inner courtyards, also paintings, prints and drawings. The Da Vinci *Mona Lisa* was displayed in a secure box behind a thick glass panel. I took a photograph like everyone else.

Time to move on—I maneuvered my luggage from the hotel to the train station. The reason for being in Europe was to show my art in an exhibit in nearby Basel, Switzerland. The bullet train provided a fast transition to that other city.

Inconceivably, the four-wheel Spinner suitcase was only a gleam in someone's eye.

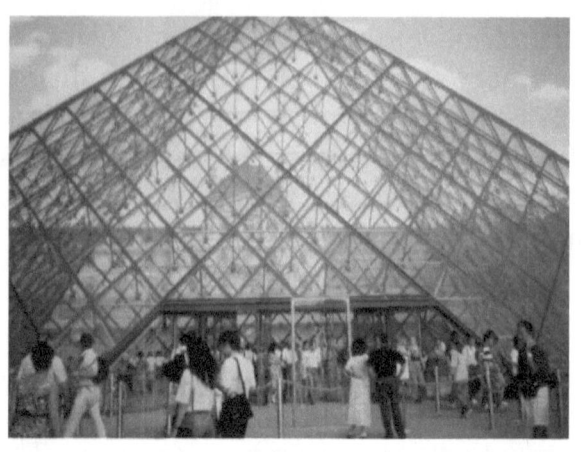

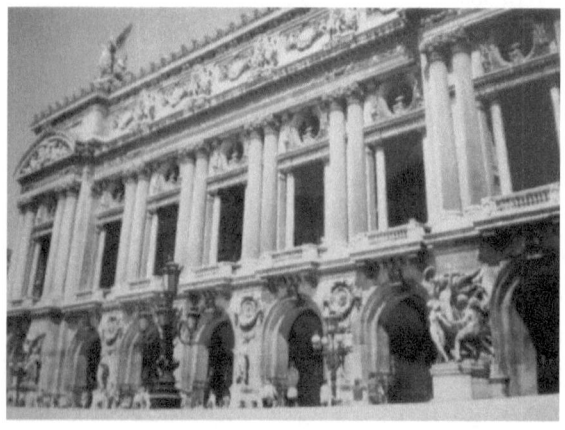

I'm Older than I've Ever Been (a few thoughts on aging)

"The realization that I may have only a few good years remaining has hit me with real force and I have done a lot of thinking as a result. I would have liked to have come up with something profound, but I haven't." That's how author Nora Ephron began the chapter in her memoir titled *The "O" Word*.

O, of course, stands for old. It's unlikely I have anything *profound*, as the author wished, to add to the aging conversation. Still, I do have plenty of feelings about it.

I have become consumed with the realization that the majority of my years are behind me. Doors have closed to a lot of opportunities that were once there: Art career moments I might have had, travels I might have experienced and places I might have lived. These paths not taken and the choices left behind elicit a feeling of melancholy with a sense of resignation.

I've surrendered to the fact that I have no lofty expectations of myself anymore. My ego has been downsized. I no longer think I will be famous, happily married or participating in the Senior Olympics, and I'm pretty much OK with all of that. I can't relate to career building opportunities anymore or life-in-the-fast-lane. The word fast doesn't describe any part of my life.

On the other hand, I feel no deprivation when I think of myself and friends who have sustained interests as we become mindful elders: artists, dancers, writers, speakers, teachers, readers, leaders, gardeners, caretakers, political and human rights activists and sagers. Growing old as they say beats the alternative, but growing old is much more than just not being dead.

So in grappling with numbered days, I'm aware that I appreciate the people and world around me, I stay very engaged with my art and community activities. I'm pondering the time ahead with some anxiety, but mostly with anticipation.

In his memoir, author Tom Robbins—87 years old—says: "I've had a messy life. But in the tangle, I think the silver thread of spirituality, the red thread of passion and of course, the elastic and multicolored thread of imagination have constantly run through it. And all of that is bound together with the inky thread of writing."

Amen to that.

PART THREE
OH, YES I DID

Going Under with a Hat

"Most of what we do in worldly life is geared toward our staying dry, looking good, not going under." —Anne Lamott

The way I remember it, I showed up at church with my homework paper bobby-pinned to my scalp because I forgot my scarf. Girls and women were obliged to wear hats in the Catholic Church, and the first time I learned about the need for head covering I was in first grade at my parochial school. Little did I know that hats would be a test of my faith.

Most mornings I walked to the school/church complex, always with a chapel veil at hand to avoid being chastened by the Dominican Sisters. We didn't question why girls had to cover their heads or why boys didn't; observing the nuns, cloaked from head to toe, the girls readily accepted the tradition.

Easter bonnets were my favorite. I liked the stylish part of hat wearing but not the overbearing, committing-a-sin, going-to-hell part of it. I felt pretty sure God didn't care, one way or the other, what was on my head. That craziness followed the notion that God was troubled if I didn't eat fish on Friday.

Even though I questioned dogma, some of the memorable features about the church were the solemn, choreographed processions in the sanctuary. The girls wore pastel dresses and floral tiaras. On any given holy day, I marched up and down the aisles with my classmates, in and out of the pews chanting Latin.

One particular religious event, the church ladies made ruffled crowns with tiny roses for us to wear in our hair. After the service we were instructed to keep them for the next day's ceremony. Sunday morning came around, but by then I had lost my hat. Yet, I knew for a fact I had to be in the procession because the nuns commanded obedience, protocol and decorum. Panic set in. I had to remake my crown. Eventually, my homemade hat consisted of cut-up cereal-box-cardboard covered in Kleenex tissues embellished with hand-picked daisies. I carefully put it all together with glue and tape, and then pinned it to my hair. No one would notice the difference.

Somewhere in the middle of the procession my crown began to fall apart. First the daisies dangled in my face, and then the tissue slipped off the cardboard, revealing a bowl of Frosted Flakes. The thought of going to hell was preferable to the humiliation I felt as I imagined all eyes on me. I wanted to be invisible.

Not having a lot of choices, I eventually surrendered to the moment and continued my march as if nothing had happened. I was six. Stubbornly, I just knew these kinds of things would perversely occur in my life and I knew endurance would be the key to not going under— with or without a hat.

Unleash the Power?

What could go wrong with a power seminar? I asked myself that question often before signing up for the weekend intensive. As soon as I entered the room that morning and was asked to stand on a chair and sing along to Tina Turner's "Simply the Best, Better than All the Rest" with several thousand people, I was out of my comfort level.

On that Friday morning in 1998, I was in downtown Denver to meet Tony Robbins, self-help author and motivational speaker. He promised that "One weekend will change everything." The promotional materials claimed we could gain the competitive edge: a connection with people, passion and the environment that will make it happen. UNLEASH THE POWER WITHIN was the title of the course. To experience a mid-art-career boost, I signed up for the weekend. I hoped for a competitive edge in the competing art world. Nothing ventured, nothing gained, I told myself.

Tony ran on stage, all 6'7" of him, throwing his arms in the air. He appeared the most outgoing, self-assured, loud, energetic speaker I had seen. Like a rock concert, we had been prepped to enthusiastically greet him. His huge smile and good looks projected onto a big screen allowed him to appear bigger than life and happy to be there. The audience loved him.

We spent the first day listening to Tony talk about passion and power. I listened, took notes and observed with the rest of the seekers. I hardly noticed the unremarkable, windowless convention center room crowded with plastic chairs. I felt optimistic and figured this was doable. Even though I had been warned of the possible amped-up atmosphere.

The second day we practiced power techniques: exercises to engage our nervous system, like standing on chairs, lying on the floor and talking to our neighbors. We learn more when we are engaged, explained Tony. As clever as he is, he wasn't able to distinguish between divergent personality learning traits. Nor did he care, but I cared because I was falling behind in the extroverted department.

Yet I was impatient for what he called the "breakthrough that transforms everything."

That afternoon the doors were locked from the inside to keep us in and focused. Locked doors seemed unnecessary, illegal and uncomfortable. Loud music, dancing and constant interactions for days felt excessive.

I had had enough. I walked to the locked doors and demanded to be let out. They refused. I insisted—they refused again.

While I practiced deep breathing, the darkened auditorium exploded with frantic chants. Tony had pumped up the crowd to "fire walk"— a practice used to boost self-confidence. If you can walk across a bed of hot coals you can do anything, he enthused. Finally the doors burst open.

Relieved to be outside, I watched the mind-over-matter crowd sprint across the hot coals in the parking lot. I passed. The late summer evening was warm as I drove home, feeling content that burnt feet would not be part of my power weekend.

The next morning, my initial eagerness was gone. Some of the group felt buoyed by their fire walk—although the crowd seemed much smaller. By noon it was over. Most, I think, believed Tony delivered what he offered: a power shift and personality adjustment to embrace the extroverted ideal.

For me it wasn't the seminar's message of passion and personal power that put me off, but the manner in which we were invited to learn. I found myself wondering, for years, if I could have participated differently—a way that wouldn't have made me wrong, but would have propelled me to a journey of discovery.

Foolhardy or Fearless

Infatuation was the only explanation I had. Under different circumstances, I wouldn't be willing to hop a freight train. But there we were, hunkered in the rail yard waiting out of sight, for the Union Pacific to come through Denver with an open boxcar or a flatbed to sneak onto. The year was 1978.

Those days it didn't take much to interest me in an adventure. But I had to wonder—how safe could this be? Nonetheless, my companion and his train-obsessed college buddies dazzled me about the fun we were going to have on a freight-hop through the Rocky Mountains.

Willingly, dressed in old jeans, sweatshirt and a borrowed hat that read Burlington Northern, we caught the coal train as it clattered and shuddered out of town. We positioned ourselves at the rear end of a Hopper car in a niche exposed to the weather and yard detectives. Our freight car wasn't designed for passengers, but it grudgingly accepted us on the cold steel platform. Too late to change my mind.

Our intrepid train left the city rail yards about 10:30 that morning. The mountains, generally a sight to behold, displaying fields of yellow aspen and snow tipped peaks rushed by as I tried in vain to get comfortable perched precariously over the rail wheels. My sweaty palms grasped hold. Hours later, cold from the rain and windburned, with the sound of rails hammering in my head, we arrived at our western stop. At an altitude of 7,000 feet, we set up camp overnight at a wooded freight-station site. The fresh mountain air couldn't soothe my apprehension of the return trip.

The next morning, we sped down the mountain pass on a flatbed of the Rio Grande Railroad in the relentless high-altitude sun, buffeted by the constant wind, surviving the cars' jarring and shaking that threatened to bounce us off. Despite the inconvenience, we had planned ahead and packed a lunch for our six-hour ride. I endured having to pee in a can while the boys nimbly caught the wind at the back of the rail car.

We rode through the famous Moffatt Tunnel, six and half miles, holding a cloth over our faces to keep out the soot and oily stench of the engine. We emerged out the other side to be greeted by onlookers, from an historic site, pointing at the *girl hobo*. They cheered. That lifted my spirits. Still, I wanted them to know that I preferred a Manhattan on a passenger train.

Almost home.

That evening, Denver never looked so good. I nursed a nasty cut on my leg from rolling down a hill after jumping off the slow-moving train hissing to a stop. It would be a while before I let anyone know how uncomfortable that trip was. Mostly I spent some time bragging about our fearless adventure.

I guess there was a place in his heart for my clumsy attempt at train-hopping, but my own heart knew I had a lapse in judgment. Here's what I tell myself: the only things I got out of that reckless trip were a good story and a relationship.

Rocky Mountain High (Aspen, Colorado 1978)

"Rocky Mountain High" was playing in the Jerome Bar, the social centerpiece of a town known for its ski slopes, affluence and celebrity sightings of actors and politicians.

Aspen is situated at the base of Aspen Mountain in the Elk Mountain Range at 8,000 feet. It was a clear fall day. I'd come here with a woman friend, driving three hours from Denver to attend an environmental conference. We rented rooms in a modestly priced inn and left our luggage unpacked—we were eager to get outside.

It was one of those perfect days.

Trees swayed with golden leaves; the sky was an intense blue with clusters of white clouds. The Valley was singing with breezes, and inside the best bar this side of the Rocky Mountains, a group of us bonded over environmental protection and being young in Aspen.

We walked to the Jerome Bar on East Main Street. Home to ski bums, socialites and cowboys, it had a genuine saloon atmosphere. The wood floors, one-hundred-year-old mahogany bar, crown molding and antique furnishings reminiscent of the Colorado Silver Boom whiffed of stale beer and cigarette smoke.

We grabbed a seat at the bar, ordered margaritas and bumped into singer/songwriter John Denver sipping a beer and singing along to his own song. I don't remember who spoke first, but anyone would have recognized him: round face, large round glasses, sandy straight hair and a cowboy hat. It was the mid 70s, and Rocky Mountain High had gone to the top of the charts - he was inspired to write the song after moving to the Aspen Valley.

The singer bought us another round of drinks and the conversation was relaxed while we were taken in by his friendly smile. He was passionate about his music, the environment and the snow-covered valley of his new home, and that's mostly what we talked about. Eventually we moved to a table in the middle of the room—my friend and I, and John and his buddy.

People walked in and out of the bar not paying any attention to us. Locals were used to seeing him there. We continued to talk and drink the rest of the afternoon while ignoring the impact of the thin air on alcohol consumption. Eventually, the perfect afternoon turned to evening and we said goodbye. Or that's the way I remember it in a blurry haze.

John Denver has been dead now for twenty years as a result of flying his plane into Monterey Bay. But every time I hear "Rocky Mountain High," "Annie's Song" or "Sunshine on my Shoulders," it takes me back to Aspen's J-Bar and spending an afternoon in the mountains with a man who knew the joy of living and the beauty of nature.

Not a bad memory.

Solo Show

*Never regret anything that makes you smile. —
Mark Twain*

After years as a professional artist living in Denver, I took the opportunity of going back home to show my accomplishments. The situation seemed like an appalling balance of grandeur and humility. In 1999, I was 56 years old, and I had just finished an art exhibit where I grew up in Ohio—a hometown I rarely set foot in.

Looking back, I made that decision because I had already been around the block exhibiting my art in galleries, art centers, colleges and museums—nationally and internationally. Where was there to go but to the past?

I contacted an Ohio museum, one I had visited as a child, and I proposed an art show. I also offered a community outreach component: I would teach both an adult and a student workshop while I was there.

After a short time, the museum invited me to have a one-woman show, and the local papermill and several small businesses accepted my proposal for funding. I was on my way. But the journey had just begun: the written proposal, the professional art photos and the grant proposal were just the tip of this excursion.

The next step was to pack up 50-100 pieces of art—all of them three dimensional, different sizes and fragile. I routinely packed up pieces to ship to a gallery now and then, but that many pieces started to feel like trouble. Everyone helped: my friends looked for large odd-shaped boxes that I could cut up and resize. Each piece felt more complicated to pack than the next. Eventual success hinged on how well I crated the art and packed the art supplies. I felt neurotic amid a sea of boxes and the acrid smell of cardboard. It took months.

Finally I called UPS for pickup, and they took it all away. I felt relieved yet apprehensive about the boxes bouncing around in the back of the van.

After a few grueling days, I got confirmation that everything arrived safely and then I flew to Ohio to help unpack. I supervised and labeled each box with repacking instructions. I thought I was finished with boxes.

Hanging the show was time consuming, but it went relatively well.

As part of my exhibit, I conducted a free workshop for students and hung their paper-pulp paintings with mine in the gallery. Every workshop I taught had its own temperament, particularly with kids—but they were an eager, talented group hand-picked by each school for their skill. Unexpectedly, my young niece arrived with the flu and unwittingly shared it with me. The two-day adult workshop was exhausting yet remarkable.

By then we were all eager to see the show.

It was May. Amid the surrounding, budding trees, the museum unfurled a 15-foot banner on the exterior of the building announcing...me. A radio interview and a newspaper interview the following day kept me on my toes. I felt exhilarated about how this was all coming together.

Opening night finally arrived. However, what I had been waiting for was about to be eclipsed by the stomach flu. I was sick.

This wasn't how I imagined it would be. Even so, the show must go on. I arrived sweaty and flushed, but I greeted people as they arrived. I managed to surreptitiously run outside for air and then to the restroom when I could. I kept that up for a couple of hours while enjoying compliments, receiving flowers and entertaining people I hadn't seen since high school. My family was proud. I was nauseated.

The next day in bed I had time to read the reviews in the local papers. The *Tribune* carried a flattering article characterizing me as "a former resident and world-renowned artist." Other town papers also were full of praise: "You won't want to miss this exciting exhibit by an internationally acclaimed and locally grown artist."

I accepted their flattery even though it wasn't true—simply their interpretation of my resume. Yet I got what I came for...hometown girl makes good.

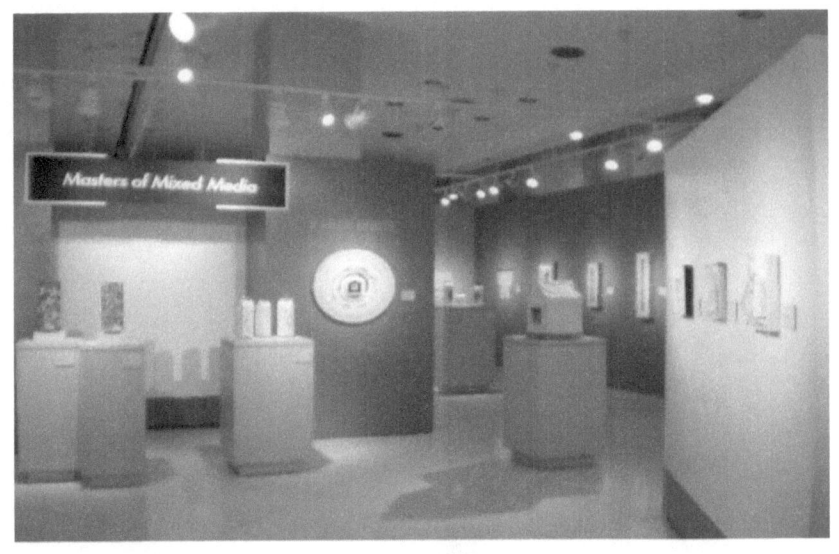

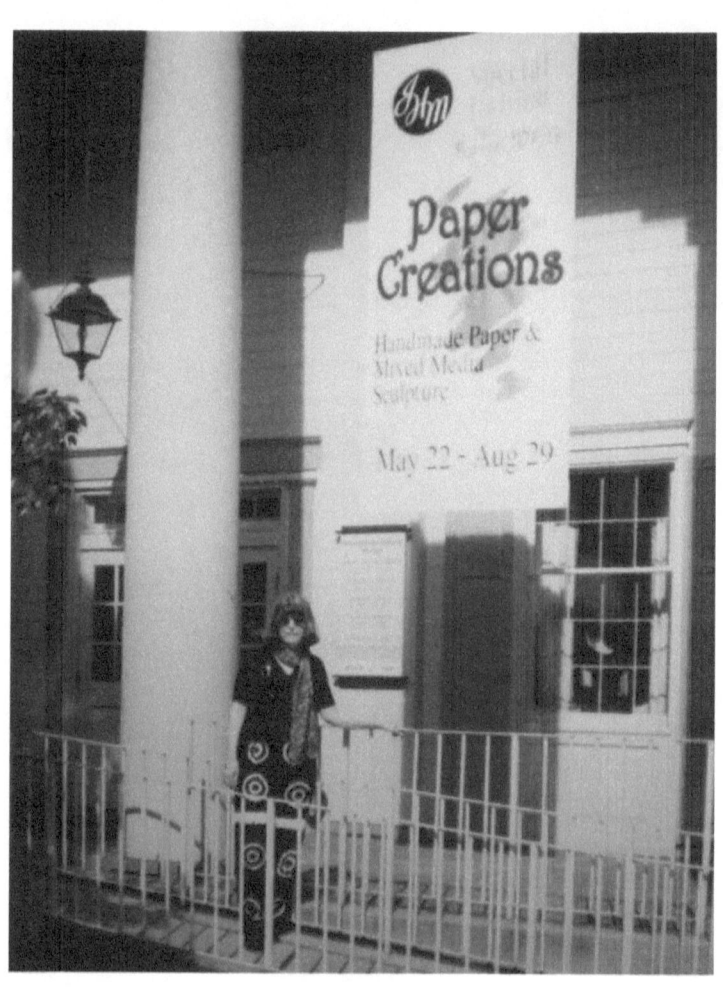

Overcoming Indecision

A few years ago, I painfully recognized I needed to buy a chair that elevates my feet and supports my back. I know they call those chairs recliners, but I'm not inclined to admit I need one. Besides, I don't like to shop because I can't make decisions.

This inability to just pick something and be happy is crippling. Nothing ever seems to be a clear choice for me, I'm always looking for the perfect solution. I can overthink a situation so much that nothing happens. And that's what happened: I remained chairless for a year.

During that time I occasionally checked online self-help features about the psychology of indecision.

Most articles agreed that "fear is the root of indecision" and that worry differs from one person to another. Some of the discomfort could be fear of responsibility, social pressure or change and certainly fear of failure.

I was looking for a simpler approach, like the five-steps-to-complete-and-easy-decision-making. Instead I found needless assertions: people worry about what hardship might follow from a wrong decision. Well, yes, exactly! And what is my way around that? The report advised only that "continued hardships are just opportunities for me to grow."

Another online suggestion: in a moment of indecision I could start a log and record my feelings. Or: I could forget the problem and relax. That review offered me a meditation-made-easy website. I had a hard time choosing between *White Noise or Rainy Mood*.

Probably my favorite decision-making suggestion was the use of an app on my tablet. Yes, there's an app for that. My choices were several, but two stood out. One called the *Decision Buddy*, at the Google store, walks me through the resolution process. The other called the *Ultimate Decision Maker* randomly picks one for me. I haven't tried either yet.

The only advice I followed was the *Deadline*. I set a deadline and forced myself under a time crunch. That made me nervous, though.

Nevertheless, I went shopping. I looked, tested and agonized over finding the perfect recliner. I had to decide on traditional, modern or Scandinavian design; leather or fabric; manual lever or sensor.

Eventually I settled on a chair and waited five weeks to have it custom upholstered, sized to fit me and delivered. At last, the cinnamon-colored chair fit perfectly in my living room with all my art.

Unfortunately, the next day I knew I was severely allergic to the chair—I had every symptom of overexposure to a chemical. The fabric was off-gassing fumes.

I returned the chair.

Tragically, I had to start all over deciding what to buy, with the fear of failure fresh in my mind. I wish I'd gained some insight into overcoming indecision the first time I bought the chair. Instead I'm looking at another website that promises to deliver Eleven Principles for Problem Solving and Good Decision Making at DontBeStupid.club.

A Little Chocolate Now and Then Doesn't Hurt

Lately, I've begun to think about which body parts I wanted to save: my heart, my mind or my joints. Books I had been reading talked about the importance of nutrients to cure all ills. To feel optimally healthy, I studied the foods that are good for me and the foods never to be eaten. By the time I finished researching, I wondered which expert to rely upon.

Recently I read *Prevent and Reverse Heart Disease* by Dr. Esselstyn, a noted cardiologist with a popular book. The food rules were these: no meat or fish, no dairy, no oil or nuts; acceptable foods were most vegetables and whole grains. This seemed limited but doable. I gave it a try.

Then I saw a PBS program featuring the *Brain Change* book that talked about how I could reduce the inflammation in my brain and stay mentally sharp as I age. The guidelines were these: eat lots of fish, nuts, oil and dairy—and limit the carbs.

This selection appeared to be the opposite of my heart-healthy diet. Already feeling that the experts were giving me a sort of Sophie's Choice about which "child" to save, I pressed on nevertheless.

I went online to investigate what foods are good for reducing arthritis symptoms. I considered that perhaps, being pain-free was more important than mental clarity or having a regular heartbeat.

This diet fell between the other two with no meat or fish, no mushrooms, spinach, asparagus or beans. No alcohol, sugar, or dairy. Too confusing, I concluded.

Looking at all the advice, I should have known better than to get caught up in the latest "you can save your life" diet. I believe the suggestions are good until the next provable diet bumps them off the must-read charts. Coffee and chocolate used to be carcinogens. Now they are lauded for a healthy diet. I let go of my research.

So to celebrate my liberation I bought two pies—a pumpkin and a blueberry. And I ate them along with a bag of sweet potato corn chips.

Charles Schultz once said, "All you need is love, but a little chocolate now and then doesn't hurt."

Celebration of Life

I wish that when the time comes we could all join hands and rush into the surf together. —Abigail Thomas

"Dead but not forgotten." The way the preacher said it really didn't have anything to do with my mother. He was given the task of her eulogy without knowing anything about her: thus, a generic tribute. She always said if you want something done right, you have to do it yourself.

Recently a group of us in the Sage-ing program decided to get out ahead of that day when we need a service, and to plan our own memorial. At first the project seemed like a benign task, just another thing to accomplish, but the more I thought about it—it felt a little weird. I carried on, though.

In getting with the program I started out by selecting a few pieces of music: Leonard Cohen's "Hallelujah," Judy Collins' "Who Knows Where the Time Goes?"—and my favorite: "That's Life," sung by James Brown. I got a little teary-eyed when I played them. I have a Mary Oliver poem that's guaranteed to make everyone weep. That's the point, isn't it? Laugh or cry...emotions need to find a path.

Such is the reality of putting together end of life matters. I have all my directives in place and the next phase of planning is a celebration of life, as some like to call it.

Our group assembled an array of information that deals with the subject. One interesting pamphlet titled Creating Peace of Mind focuses on how to organize our last wishes—this was clearly for our families' peace of mind. My grandfather's situation is a case in point—he left absolutely nothing in writing about his wishes when he died. My mother felt challenged.

We looked at another collection called Scripting our Last Moments on Earth. The purpose is to increase our awareness of the reality of physical death. We wondered how much more aware we should be. This one suggested creating a skit and acting out our memorial service. I'm not quite there on that one—I'm an introvert.

Probably the most useful few pages of advice are "How to Plan a Memorial Service." It includes a 17-point checklist for decision making. Some of the considerations are location, flowers, music, speaker, catering, photograph, a printed program and the obituary. The plan mentioned that if you find the list daunting, consider hiring a funeral director or event planner. That states the obvious, I think. I'm still baffled by item number three on their list that encouraged us to "Select a Date." I told the group I was uncomfortable with that one. I can't picture myself sending out "save the date" notices.

After considering all the possibilities I'm still struggling with how I want a modest memorial to look—somewhere between an undistinguished service like my mother's and event-planner-extravagant. Meanwhile, I will move right along to writing my obituary—which, I think, will have two lines and four words and say:

Loved art
 Ate chocolate.

PART FOUR
WHO COULD HAVE KNOWN?

Draw Me!

On the back page of my comic book, bold black letters jumped out at me: **"Can You Draw This?"** scrawled under a portrait of a young woman. Feeling like this might be an opportunity to prove my talent, I decided to answer the ad, but I worried they wouldn't like me as much as I liked the idea of being discovered. Did I mention that I was thirteen?

During the 1950's "Draw Me" and "Do You Like To Draw?" advertising campaigns were on the back page of comic books and on most matchbook covers. The ads encouraged the viewer to sketch a "draw me" figure: a woman, a movie star or a cartoon character—then answer a few questions and mail the drawing to Minnesota. Newspaper and magazine advertising at that time were illustrated, not photographed, thus the search around the country for artistic talent. I wanted to be part of it.

The only art on our walls at home were a couple of framed flower paintings. My personal collection of art consisted of several Constable prints (copies, of course) that I kept in a drawer. In school, without a chance for art classes, the nuns regularly chose me to create the tedious homeroom decorations. Our small town offered me nothing—I couldn't wander into an art gallery or museum for inspiration. I was on my own.

Despite the lack of opportunity, I had some early ambition and willingly looked outside the area for validation. Was the back page ad of a comic book my portal?

I sat down with white typing paper and a #2 pencil and then drew a portrait of the young woman pictured in the comic book advertisement. The side view showed her long neck, perfect heart-shaped lips and coiffed hair. In my explicit exactness I aced the illustration, although it seemed entirely too easy to be any kind of test. I stuffed my art piece into an envelope and mailed it. Then I waited.

After the company received my "draw me" submission along with our home address, it was turned over to a representative who drove from town to town looking for a sales opportunity. One summer afternoon while I was home alone, the agent made his way to my door. I hesitantly invited him in. Sitting at our dining room table, business-like in a white shirt, he announced I had passed the "talent test." What a relief! I waited for him to continue the favorable critique. No such luck. He quickly became assertive and impatient while asking if I could afford three hundred dollars for the art course.

Well, of course I couldn't, I told him, feeling a knot in my stomach as my shoulders slumped. I saw my young art career slipping away on that summer day. I'm sure he noticed that small-town Ohio and our cluttered home was no hotbed of artistic significance. He moved on.

Although I followed my instincts, I don't know exactly what I had hoped by answering the ad—it stood to reason that I could count on a legitimate assessment of my talent, instead I got a salesman. In hindsight, the situation seemed to be a forerunner for the high expectations and the letdowns of the art world that I was to spend the rest of my life navigating.

Field Trip Fervor

It's only a dim memory, but I believe the local Ohio history museum was five blocks from Sacred Heart Catholic School. My grade school class took a field trip there—a repurposed two-story stone schoolhouse with a bell tower

The nuns lined us up two by two in a long column for our walk to Sycamore Street. We walked across the school playground and down Main Street, past the stone-clad Post Office and the American Legion hall. The Library commanded the corner of Fourth and Chestnut Street. There were large, leafy Maple trees that lined our walkway and red brick streets. All were familiar sights, usually seen from our family car or on my walk to the Saturday afternoon movies.

But somehow everything looked out-of-the-ordinary walking, with a sense of purpose, to discover the history of our town. We gazed at the sullen museum. A few scraggly trees stood in front. It looked haunted. But we approached with wonderment.

I have a memory of creaky wood floors and small, poorly lit rooms crammed with aged photos and dusty costumes. The Native American room, on the first floor—stuffed to the gills with colorful, textural artifacts— felt sacred. This was our history— the Delaware Indians. A display across the room had communal items the tribe crafted:

woven grass baskets, clay beads, necklaces of sun bleached animal bones and chiseled slate arrowheads. These all formed our history and a mystery that I could only imagine. Our visit didn't seem long enough.

The unforgettable part of our outing was not the museum, but a manufacturing plant called The Dairy a block away. We hustled to the factory where we could buy cones, sundaes and shakes. They had an ice cream parlor with a spectacle of flavors displayed in a silver refrigerated case.

Did I make a mistake by straying from chocolate? My selection, a black raspberry ice-cream cone, did me in that day. It tasted funny. I ate it and dealt with the consequences.

Fifty years later I had an art exhibit at that historic museum— now in a new location. I remember the show well: I caught the stomach flu from kids who had come for a field trip and a workshop. My lingering and inconvenient stomach distress would be a memorable part of my art show.

Sometimes you just can't get away from the past because life is a succession of moments to be remembered—like it or not.

Cross Signals

The town I grew up in had trains coming and going, day and night, and we had to learn to live with them. And that's why I was often at the crossing, with crossing-guard warning lights flashing and bells clanging while the Baltimore & Ohio rolled into town. I could feel the endless sequence of cars vibrate beneath my feet. I wanted to back away, but I didn't. I always stood my ground like the big kids.

Trains were fearsome giants, I thought. Like a bully, the locomotive overwhelmed the small town. During the day it blocked traffic on Main Street, inconveniencing everyone until it was ready to roll away.

In the evening I heard the familiar night cries of the freight trains, just a few blocks from my house down a thicket covered hill. It was a different whistle—more like a caution.

This was the generation of the rail-yard hobo in the 1940s and 50s. Men jumped out of empty box cars and bummed around looking for handouts or a day's work. Eventually, the hobos made their way into our neighborhood searching for a meal. Everyone called them tramps: unshaven, with worn-out shoes and torn, dirty shirts that revealed tattoos. Sometimes they appeared at our back screen door looking sad and threatening. My mother never turned them away. But not wanting to invite them in, she fed the men on our back porch steps. Strangers ate from our china as I watched from the safety of the window.

Before leaving, they marked our porch with an "X" signifying to their fellow vagabonds, my mother said, that this was a good place for a handout. I knew to leave that "X" in place: it signaled that our family would be spared any hobo retaliation.

My mother understood that they were traveling workers. In my mind they were a mysterious lot communicating with each other by way of chalked "hobo signs" on fences, buildings and trees.

I wouldn't go outside the rest of the evening. I lay in bed comforted by the sound of the resonating rails as the train left town.

Denver, Colorado

In the summer of 1972 I headed west from Columbus to Denver because the western climate was dry and the temperatures were moderate. I wanted out of the Midwest humidity. I packed the beat-up Dodge Rambler and drove four days and 2200 miles with an old boyfriend. I had never seen anything like the Rocky Mountains.

I can't just pick one story to recount my time there. I've listed a few impressions about the city: clean, artistic, and progressive, with delightful restaurants, attractive architecture (Queen Anne houses dotting the city), intriguing Silver Boom and Gold Rush history and wonderful friends.

I liked it there. I liked the cultural activities, the vast park systems in the city and the healthy lifestyle people exhibited. I didn't like the temperature inversions that trapped dirty air over the city, causing a brown cloud on most days. Because of the sad state of the air quality in Denver, I quickly joined the local environmental group in 1979. Thus started my interest in preserving and strengthening the National Clean Air Act.

Denver had a thriving art community, and I immediately landed a gallery to showcase my work in the prestigious Cherry Creek area. Then I branched out to other exhibit venues while I taught part-time at a local community college. The Mile High City was a good hub for distributing and shipping my art to exhibits around the country and to some international destinations as well.

I worked with a great group of women to establish the Women's Art Center and Gallery for local artists. The Center was a hub for popular community art projects, multi-media art shows, music and readings.

My then partner and I bought a run-down, turn-of-the-century corner grocery store in 1980. We completely renovated it into a living space, art studio and office for his contractor business. We lived and worked there until our divorce in 1998. I stayed several more years and turned the space into a gallery to showcase my art, along with works by other local artists. In 2010 I sold the building and moved to Winter Haven, Florida. I never looked back.

Crack in the Night

A deafening explosion yanked me up out of a sound sleep. I mumbled to my then husband that someone had just firebombed our neighbors. He looked at me. "I don't think it was our neighbors," he said. Just then we could see a fog of dust coming through the doorway, clouding our vision and reeking of burnt rubber and fumes.

I have trouble sleeping and routinely wake up every two hours just to make sure I'm still here. There are many reasons for this sleeplessness. Even though I usually attribute everything to old age, that's not how it started: thirty years ago a truck crashed into my newly renovated home/studio and left a gaping hole.

My husband and I had just moved in at Third and Delaware. We spent almost three years refurbishing an 1890s brick grocery store into a beautiful studio/office/loft space. Mysteriously, the building stood for nearly 100 years and no one had run into it—until then. I took it personally. Maybe the impertinence of its renewal angered the gods. With new paint, plumbing, wiring, new walls, windows, doors and roof, new trees, sod and sidewalks the space had been meant for a showplace and a home. We were proud.

I didn't particularly want to live in that area, but I did want to live in this building that we bought. The inner city was part gentrified and part Wild

West. Parts of downtown Denver resembled its rugged history.

It was early spring—the leaves hadn't quite formed on the trees. I remember because one of our newly planted honey-locusts had gotten sideswiped that night. In the quiet darkness, while the whole neighborhood slept, a drunk driver lost control of a stolen truck and slammed into our building...crashing through the brick wall.

I saw dust rising and bricks falling amid a jumble of burst drywall, splintered wood, electrical wire and furniture. Brick dust powdered the floor and covered the truck cab that looked out of place in the middle of the room. The driver scrambled away, never to be found.

After we attended to the police reports and the tow truck, we boarded up the hole to keep us secure until daylight. I couldn't sleep that night. The next day we dealt with the insurance company, contractors, curious neighbors and helpful friends. Eventually, our place was on the road to repair, but I wasn't.

I made futile attempts, night after night, to sleep, but my nervous system was sensitive to the slightest sound. I tried sleeping in different parts of the building away from the street—nothing helped. Over the years other circumstances have compounded the problem. Eventually, I realized interrupted sleep was my new normal. Nowadays, at three in the morning—I listen to recorded books, or have a snack and do some writing. I've learned to make valuable use of the gaps in my night.

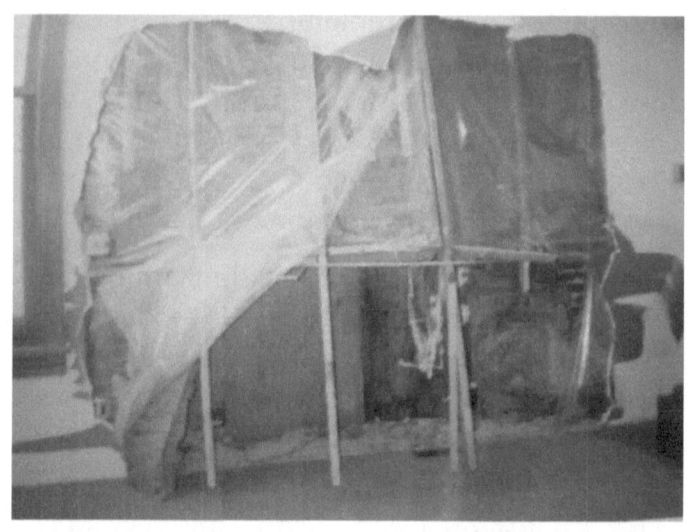

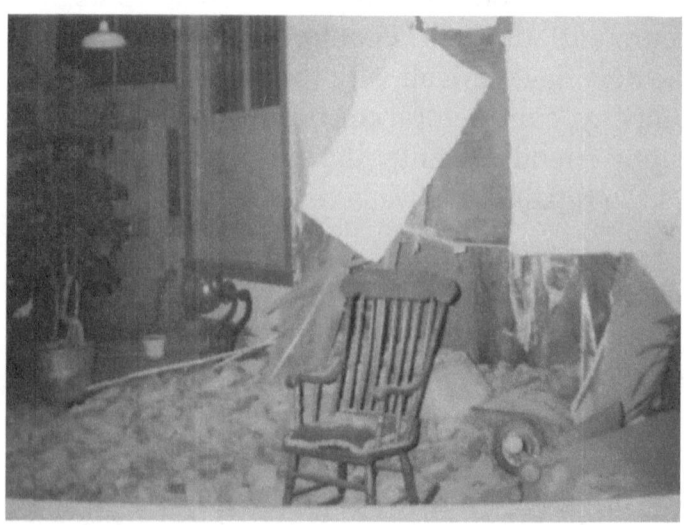

Art Studio 1985-2008 (Denver)

Inspiration is for amateurs, the rest of us just show up and get to work. — Chuck Close

It's hard to say how much of the pleasure I had working in the Denver studio was offset by frustration. Creating is always a dance of success and failure, of disappointment and elation, of being blocked and then having immense clarity. It's all part of the creative process. Author Michael Cunningham said it best: The art we anticipate is always superior to the art we can create.

My art studio was, in fact, two large rooms running north and south in our remodeled turn-of- the-century building in Denver's oldest downtown neighborhood. Situated on a corner lot surrounded by honey locust trees, flagstone sidewalks, and paint over old sand brick, the place hid its capacity and function well.

Inside, French doors indicated a division from work space to living space with the same high ceilings throughout. I would joke that I had a two-foot commute to work every day.

Large clerestory skylights, which functioned as solar collectors in the winter, spanned most of the ceiling letting in plenty of daylight. The light fell on the walls filled with art, on the tables overflowing with papermaking supplies and equipment. I choreographed my mixed media pieces: standing, moving, reaching, pushing, pulling, until the tug of intuition guided me to stop. I was always there working: on cold winter days and hot summer days.

Every supply I could possibly need I collected: paint, pencils, brushes, card stock, foam board, string, cabinets, buckets, molds, containers, knives, scissors, sponges, wood, metal, books, tools, glue, beads, wire, cameras and camera equipment. Art appeared everywhere: finished pieces and half-finished pieces, along with work set aside for a show and art waiting to be sold or shipped. Some days it felt cluttered.

At the end of the day, my time at that studio added up to dedication, lots of physical work, plenty of learning and an abundance of art.

Making art depends on that kind of commitment, a leap of faith, and a good studio.

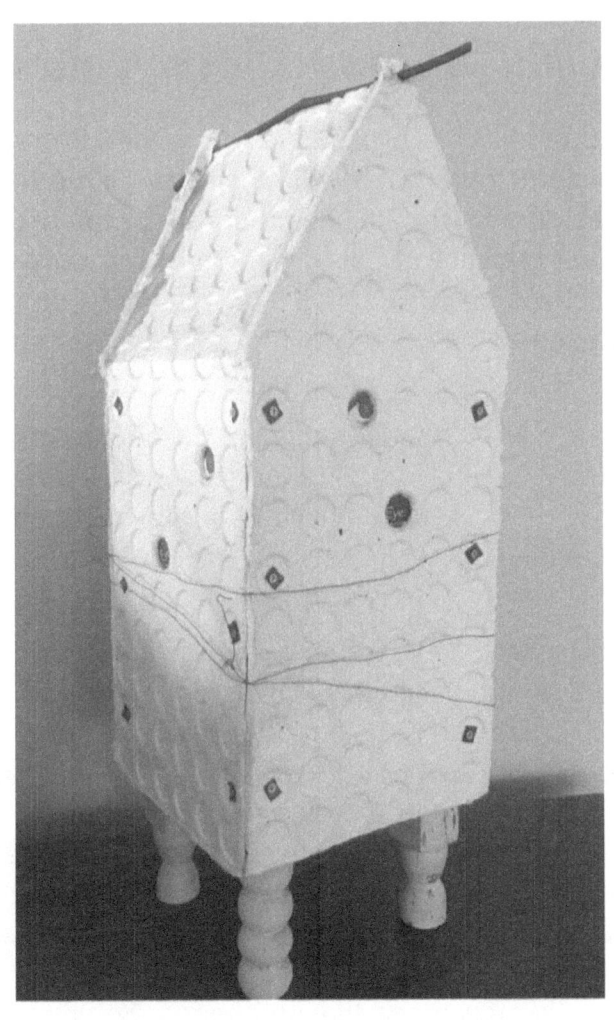

Collection of Jacqueline June

California Dreamin' (80's, 90's)

I thought I was the luckiest person in Colorado to be going to Southern California in the middle of a cold, snowy winter. I could enjoy the hot tub, the pool and the ocean. Palm trees and warm breezes all seemed a luxury to someone who grew up in Ohio and now lived at the foot of the mountains in Denver.

Every year I made the trip to Pasadena to celebrate the holidays. I grew to love spending time with my gracious in-laws because of their fun-loving nature. During our visits we made excursions in and around Los Angeles.

One year we experienced the Rose Parade hosted by the Pasadena Tournament of Roses. The extravagant flower-covered floats sailed along Colorado Boulevard on New Year's Day—we sat in the judges' grandstand. The parade seemed exaggerated—the spectacle of floats (40 of them) covered in flowers, seeds and petals processioning for two hours. Twenty marching bands strutted amid cheers from the thousands lining the sidewalks. It seemed like an illusion. Some of that opinion had to do with the "funny" brownies I ate while waiting for the parade to start. Still, it was an over-the-top pageant—anyone would agree.

I'm not very seaworthy, so I took two Dramamine before I boarded a boat to Catalina Island. A group of whales joined our boat ride "26

Miles Across the Sea." One half of one pill would have been sufficient. I recovered from my overdose at the Zane Grey Hotel (the writer's former home). The next day I planned a steep hilly ascent with my new mountain bike—a pathetic attempt on the ride up, but the ride down was swift.

On our train excursion from Los Angeles to San Francisco, we had a private compartment. The California Limited meandered up the coast and ducked behind the hills then popped up again at the ocean. We read, talked, had cocktails in the dining car and listened to stories from the seasoned train car attendants. There's no better way to travel.

Fortunately, most trips included cultural activities. The art and architecture in Southern California and the Huntington Museum, the Norton Simon Museum and the architecturally significant Mission-style Gamble house in Pasadena were crossed off my wish list. We viewed the art at the California Museum of Art and the many galleries in the Santa Monica area. This was the icing on the California cake.

In those days, I would dream of California all year long. Now I don't travel there, and I don't dream of going. Sometimes, though, I think I see a familiar palm tree silhouetted against a December moon.

Ah, Wilderness!

No one knew what was ahead on a calm, sunny, summer afternoon in the Rocky Mountains. The mountain range known as the Continental Divide cuts through the state of Colorado. In 1986, two dogs, four male friends and I hiked up the side of Grays Peak—one of the highest mountains on the Front Range known as a *fourteener*.

The state has 56 mountain peaks exceeding 14,000 feet. For many outdoor visitors, climbing a peak is a bucket-list item. The recommendation is that you be physically fit, acclimated to high altitude and smart enough to know when you're in trouble.

Three of my friends had plenty of climbing experience. As a matter of fact, they saw themselves as mountain men. Their buddy, who flew in from out-of-state, was at a disadvantage from the start.

I had hiked numerous trails and traveled the hills on my mountain bike, but I considered myself only slightly proficient in the wilderness.

We got a late start that day and had planned on a three-to-four hour hike. We drove up to 7,000 feet to the base and designated it our campsite. Our climb was rocky, sometimes grassy and somewhat gentle in places. Who could dispute the beauty of the Colorado wilderness?

Outfitted with my day-pack—food and water, rain gear, first aid kit and sunscreen—I felt prepared. Maybe I could make a mountain woman out of this city girl.

After a couple of hours on the ascent the air got thinner and I knew it would be dark soon: it was time for me to turn back. The guys were aware of my concerns, but they disagreed and tried to talk me into going further with them, not wanting to abandon me on the side of a mountain. Still they went on, ready to risk it all for a chance at reaching the top.

I took the dogs and turned around. After a few doubtful moments about my ability to find my way back alone, I hastened down the mountain with dogs in tow. I was aware of how easy it is to get disoriented. The mountains can be beautiful but dangerous places if you're lost or confused. A dose of reality hit me. Mountain woman I was not.

Nevertheless I had to get myself and the dogs to the campsite. I watered and fed the dogs—grateful for their company. I ate a granola bar and rested a few minutes. The sun had disappeared behind the mountain top. I had to move fast. There were no other climbers in sight. The dogs followed me eagerly. Just then I experienced a sense of complete aloneness amid the vast expanse of nature. I still had an hour's hike ahead of me.

Eventually, I saw the camper-top sticking out among the pines. The doggies and I were exhausted, but safe.

Darkness had settled on my friends up in the hills. Had they turned back or were they still determined to reach the top? I had no way of knowing. I figured the Californian was probably in trouble by now.

The blackness surrounded me. I saw a million stars in the sky, but the stars couldn't illuminate the mountain to aid lost climbers. I watched for hours. I felt angry—they knew better than to get caught on the trails after dark with no significant light. But there were risk-takers in these hills, something I'd seen more than once.

Somehow I wanted to help this group get safely down the mountain, but how? I decided to orient the Volkswagen van to point toward the trail, and then I began to flash the headlights every few minutes.

Time crawled by as I flashed the lights and watched for a signal from them. And then I saw it—a dim flicker of a light followed by voices. They had made it back, but not without consequences. Their non-acclimated buddy was suffering from hypothermia, altitude sickness and dehydration. He was confused and shaking badly. We put him into the camper, wrapped him in blankets and coats, and fed him some hot liquid. As a result of the cold mountain night, exhaustion and not being acclimated, he was in serious trouble.

We drove down the mountain to the highway. Throughout the long drive home, their friend gradually responded to the warmth of the blankets and the lower elevation. He would recover.

I'm not sure if those daring adventurers learned anything from that episode. They were on another exploit within weeks. I, however, was changed by this experience. I was humbled to realize even though people love the mountains, the mountains don't love you back. I discovered I could not be a mountain woman and I learned to trust my instincts.

Ah, Wilderness!, a play by Eugene O'Neill, has a happy ending, also, for a youthful character lacking discretion. O'Neill nevertheless wrote that "life was a wicked opportunity."

Death Valley Days

The summer temperature in 2013 broke a record in Death Valley according to the meteorologist on the Weather Channel. Over the next several weeks I watched with some interest because this brought back memories. I was no stranger to the Desert heat.

East of Los Angeles, past the San Bernardino hills, beyond the dusty small town of Barstow is the Mojave Desert. It's the southern part of Death Valley stretching across to the Nevada border. Years ago, I wondered if it was possible to drive through the desert, in the summer, during the day, without air conditioning or a cell phone. In 1982 my husband and I impetuously decided to make that trip on state route 15 from California to Colorado.

It was late summer, hot and windy, we had gone to Southern California to help his parents rebuild their house after it had burnt to the ground in one of the San Gabriel Valley wildfires. We stayed as long as we could, then decided to take the shortest way back home—through Death Valley.

To cross the desert we packed plenty of water and ice, including a spray bottle to substitute for an air-conditioning system we didn't have. I dressed lightly in shorts and a t-shirt and pulled my hair up in a clip—feeling somewhat ready for our adventure. Still, I was fearful of getting too hot and not being able to do anything about it.

Driving the truck down into the Basin toward the Mojave Desert, we immediately lost our radio reception. For the first few miles, no other cars were in sight. Heat lifted from the pavement in a blistering ripple. At the last gas station, a faded tin sign warned us to have adequate fuel and water before venturing further. We didn't turn back.

It was hot. Too hot! The air was thick with heat and smelled of sage. I spritzed myself often but the water evaporated instantly when it hit my skin. The dry wind flowing in from the rolled-down windows only made us hotter. The desert unfurled flat and dry and relentless with miles of sand, cactus, rocks and rodents, plus an occasional car. Tall Joshua trees were scraggy and scattered. Sagebrush seemed to defy the sun while tumbleweeds rolled around the desert floor like large, dusty, dandelion puff balls. We kept going.

Hours later, about the time I had more misgivings and feeling overheated we mercifully made it to the other service station near the border. It was a little run down place in the middle of nowhere, but enough of a settlement that I felt reassured that I wasn't going to die in the desert. The worst was behind us. We gassed up and it seemed we couldn't drive east fast enough.

Gradually the scrub, cactus and sun disappeared as we approached Nevada. I finally felt relief as the temperature dropped—we had made it through Death Valley. I thought I would never do that trip again, but we did, during December, when the average day temperature was 65 degrees.

In hindsight, I suppose that summer trip wasn't any more harrowing than regularly driving through the Rocky Mountains, during the winter, in snow and ice, sliding around those mountain curves. Yet, I felt the label Death Valley was a formidable forecast.

Connecting the Dots

You can't connect the dots looking forward; you can only connect them looking backwards. — Steve Jobs

The truth is I lack the home decorating gene. I'll never have my condo featured in Architectural Digest or in The Florida Homes and Lifestyle magazine. When my friend Terri was here for a visit, she candidly advised me how I could make the place look more designer-y.

This prompted me to think how I might have inherited my apprehension toward home decorating.

My parents, at times, were a do-it-yourself duo. They painted our house, wallpapered the walls and repaired furniture. They made things last.

When I was about four years old, my parents painted the linoleum to give the kitchen a facelift. I'm not sure why they didn't pull up that old stuff and resurface the wood floor, but instead they scrubbed the worn-out vinyl and prepared it for a makeover.

The worst part wasn't the gray paint they selected for the linoleum. No, the worst part was their decision to stencil a pattern on the newly painted floor. One day they brought home a wooden template: it had a series of round sponges which, when dabbed in paint and stamped, produced...polka dots.

I had a little red-and-white polka dot dress that I loved. Dots made sense on a dress.

Nevertheless, they speckled the entire gray floor with white dots. The next day they did it all over again with red. The red spots fell somewhere in between the white ones, and sometimes the dots overlapped when the template slipped. The visual project was troubling. From the doorway, the spots seemed to swim before my eyes.

I'm not sure it needed a third color, yet their next selection was yellow.

The room looked both fresh and frightful. The kitchen, painted a bright lemony latex, and with the red, white and yellow dots on the floor, resembled a bounce house.

No one's perfect.

Remodeling on a budget never works unless you have the "shabby chic" flair. And I don't, although sometimes I pretend I come by it naturally.

The Purge

My decision could have been an incredible miscalculation of possibilities. At age 67 I packed up and moved from Colorado to Florida, leaving a life behind.

I chose to make the move because of the high altitude and the bad effects 5,000 feet had on me—mostly fatigue and headaches. The other reasons revolved around greener pastures, both literally and metaphorically.

Once I made that decision, I looked around my spacious studio/home and almost cried. I didn't relish the idea of purging a space I had occupied for 30 years. I knew it would take at least a year to go through my cluttered studio, the stuffed basement and massive bookshelves...and on and on. Even now I shudder when I think about it.

First I told my friends my plans and solicited their help. They were sometimes skeptical or disappointed, but they all rallied 'round for the clean-out. Even with their help I wondered at times if this was possible

My new words were downsize, dispense with and dispose of. I was ready for the dreaded clean-out and knew I had to be ruthless. I started slowly in my studio by selling all my papermaking equipment to my assistant. That was a major decision and a story of its own. Wistfully, I gave away supplies, threw away materials, and donated to schools. Some days it didn't look like I had made a dent in all the stuff. Nevertheless, I picked up the pace and moved on to the other rooms.

I gave books to anyone who would take them and then donated the rest to the library—saving only a few for myself. I practically forced friends to take the furniture, kitchenware, some art and the never-used Christmas decorations (supplied by my in-laws with good intentions).

My friends felt apprehensive, I sensed, when I let things go. They were sure I would regret my unrestrained cleansing. Yet nothing was the same after my decision to move on. I looked at everything with different eyes. Miraculously I wasn't attached to my stuff anymore.

I boxed up what I needed, a few dishes and my pared-down wardrobe. Most of my moving boxes were filled with art supplies and art pieces for prospects in my new life. Gone were my antiques, my old journals, my plants, even the potted trees that I was fond of. I sold my car and gave away coats, boots and gloves. I felt giddy and weary.

After saying goodbye to my pets buried in the backyard, I touched the bare studio walls and said, "So long."

It had been a year. I put the building on the market, and then I left town feeling hopeful I hadn't miscalculated the possibilities.

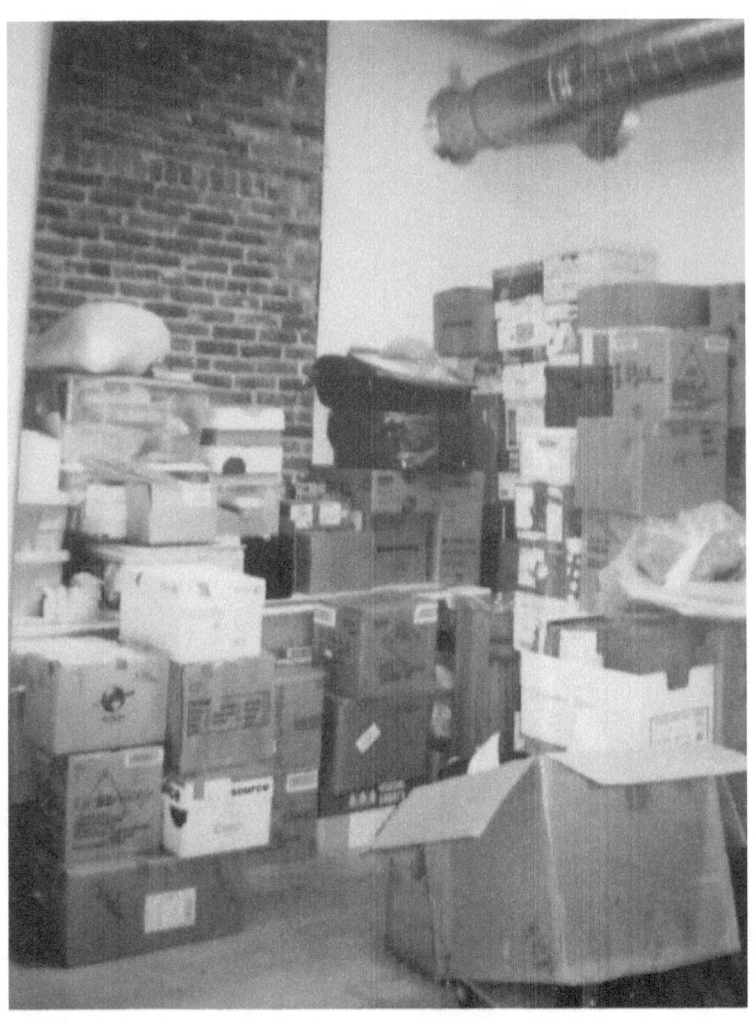

PART FIVE
TAKING A STAND

Finding My Moral Compass in the 60s

Norman Mailer wrote *Armies of the Night* in reaction to the volatile times in the 60s. President John Kennedy was assassinated in 1963, Martin Luther King was gunned down in 1968, Robert Kennedy was killed in 1968. Civil rights marches and the peace movement had a strong presence at Ohio State University beginning in 1965. I was settled-in with my art at the college, watching the nation undergoing profound changes. Because of protests and the resulting tear gas, the campus sometimes looked sinister in a foggy cloud. It was then that I saw a world of civically enlightened students, and that helped me find my moral direction.

Because I wanted peace, I joined the famous March on Washington in 1967—the national demonstration against the Viet Nam War. It was a proud moment being in the nation's capital with thousands who believed in the peace movement. Because I wanted civil rights for everyone, I also worked in freedom groups on campus. Because I wanted equality, I embraced the women's liberation movement. A vast network of people working in those groups provided lifelong human rights lessons and friendships. It was an exciting time to be young and impassioned.

While at OSU I juggled a campus job, a relationship, classes and art studio time with those moral causes. I remember worrying about the country and my future. I worried about rent, grades and tuition even though I had a job and a student loan. I worried I was overextended in work, classes and politics, but I couldn't give up on any.

Author Anne Lamott summed up my feelings well: "I was drawn to oddballs, ethnic people, theater people, poets, radicals and beat artists—and somehow they all helped me become some of those things I wanted so desperately to become: political, intellectual, artistic."

I remain convinced there are some things in life that we ought to care enough about to take a stand. I reserve the right to that sentiment because—sadly—those struggles continue to this day.

Peace out. (colloquialism of the 60s)

Road Not Taken

The saga of my clashing careers in the 60s came to mind after I watched a television show recently. In an episode of Mad Men, a 1960s period drama on cable TV, the Madison Avenue Advertising firm had just installed their first computer—a monstrous IBM 360. The firm vacated several rooms in order to fit the computer parts into their offices. That's right. One system filled an entire room with cables, components, air conditioning and vacuum tubes.

Along with this massive electronic machine came several trained programmers to set up the system for the ad firm. That I found this TV episode captivating was, of course, because I became part of that computer world in the 60s.

I had to find a way to pay for school during my college years studying fine arts at Ohio State University. IBM, a frontrunner in the computer world, offered courses for anyone daring enough to participate in a new field. I signed up for an extended curriculum. Because of my feminist nature, I believed I could do most of what men could. I was the only female to register. Looking back, I found this amusing because women were the pioneer programmers in the field, and women invented the computer punch card system—a secret kept by the industry for years. Eventually I earned an IBM certificate.

Soon the University (OSU) hired me to work, while a student, in the Computer Analytic Department. I assisted other students with the computer-peripheral equipment and their computer programming needs that related to their college courses. Although I was a fine arts student, working toward my BFA, I was adept at correlating data. The situation felt a little schizophrenic. I ran from the art building across campus every afternoon to the computer center in the business building. My bohemian appearance, mini-skirts and tights often drew good-natured comments in the office. I felt lucky to have the job.

When I graduated, the college immediately hired me to work in the Education Department to program their new modular class schedule. This job required me to fly, in the University's single engine planes, to local schools for consultation. I was terrified of such small aircraft at first, but it was another adventure that kept me hooked.

But before long I began to notice colleagues spending their weekends and evenings honing their computer skills for this fast-moving industry. I was falling behind. I spent my weekends and evenings making art. I found my clashing careers difficult to resolve day by day.

Eventually, I quit the incredibly well-paid, great-benefits job to be a full-time artist with no benefits other than satisfaction.

From time to time I think about that road not taken 50 years ago. I could have grown with the computer industry: instead, I chose to bloom with the arts. No regrets. Well, maybe some.

The Shrine Project

Art is a counterweight to lack of hope. I embraced that sentiment when I got involved with managing an inner-city art project with at-risk kids. Despite my good intentions with the task ahead, I had to navigate hurdles, both personal and public.

In 1995, I put together a proposal for a community art project. The US Justice Department was interested in seeding troubled neighborhoods with money for activities and innovation to prevent the hopelessness that could lead to crime. It was a considerable amount of work for me to design the project, to write the grant for funding, to pitch the plan to community leaders and, finally, to work with the kids for the final art piece. This would be a year-long undertaking.

At that time I was feeling a bit hopeless too, so I'm not sure why I decided to tackle this activity. My marriage had fallen apart, and I experienced some health problems. Perhaps this project would be my counterweight.

We called it the Shrine Project, or Santeros. I planned on working with youngsters to design and build individual small shrines dedicated to their family, school or church. Assembled together, the pieces would span a 6 x 10 foot wall. The project looked to be a fit for the largely Hispanic Catholic community. I was glad to have a common theme to introduce the proposal.

In spite of my enthusiasm and the general interest of the project, I was considered an outsider in the district. A few neighborhood organizers were skeptical of me, and they tried to derail the project. I felt indignant about the unwelcome. But I had to ask if it was wrong to impose my vision on the community. For a while it seemed a difficult situation. After much finagling, our Councilwoman stepped in and advocated on my behalf.

Finally getting the go-ahead, I recruited kids from public schools, the Boys and Girls Clubs, a recreational center, the churches and other neighborhood youth-oriented services. The groups included good kids, problem kids, gang-affiliated kids, and poor, neglected and hungry kids. All this, from a blighted community that remained earmarked as troublesome. Gang activity and graffiti brought city resources plus activists together trying to safeguard the neighborhood. They needed this as much as I did.

There was so much to laugh and cry about during this project. Had I really thought about it, I would have had more people helping me, especially Spanish speakers; I would have partnered with an artist from their community; I would have been more aware of my safety and I would have paid myself a lot more.

The best moments of the project had to be watching the kids enthusiastically craft their shrines. They laughed, ate snacks and worked as I admired their boundless inventiveness.

I forgot how fatigued I felt some days and went home tired but energized. Loneliness lost its edge because most days I was surrounded with project companions.

Problems popped up from time to time: a few community activists continued to voice that I had no right to be there. Sometimes the kids were too exuberant. In one case, a child was injured during an art supply fight; another time, I was ignoring the danger of the area when someone shot at my car, leaving shattered glass in the back windows of my old Volvo station wagon.

Through it all, though, I felt the experience tipped in favor of satisfaction.

Together we assembled an exceptional art piece that confirmed to me that art is a critical component in personal fulfillment, self-confidence and fun. Well received by the kids, local newspapers and the City, the Santeros Creation was displayed in the Denver City and County building, and a downtown art gallery and eventually was returned to the neighborhood.

The Shrine Project was one of many art ventures I created with that community.

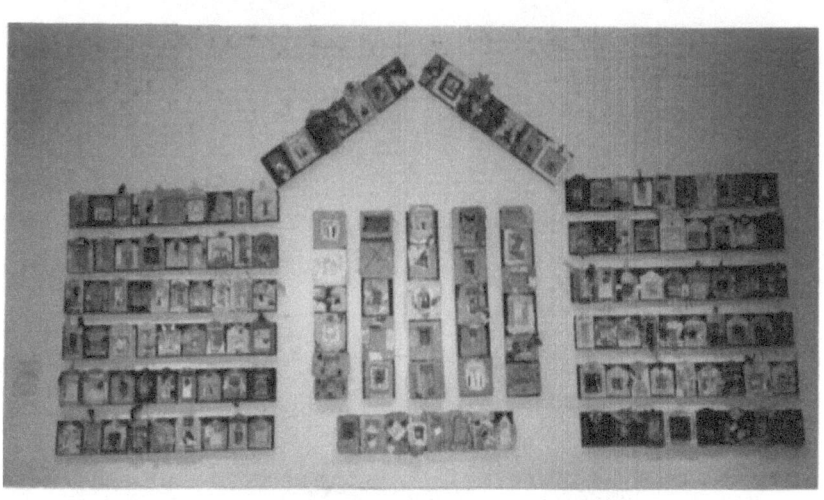

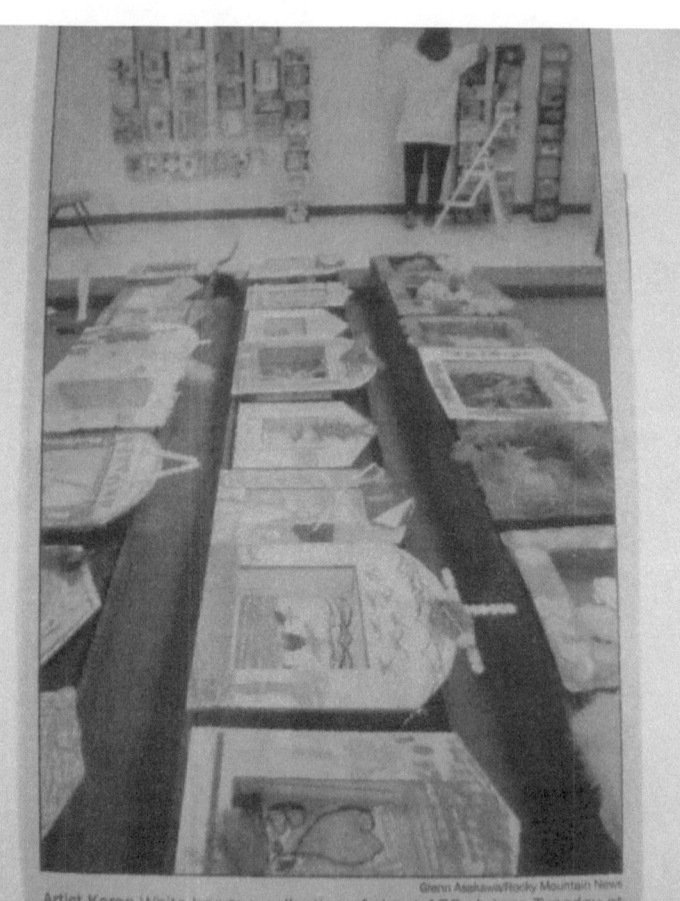

Artist Karen White hangs a collection of about 150 shrines Tuesday at the Boys and Girls Club of Metro Denver, 721 W. Eighth Ave. The shrines were made by youths and adults in the Baker and La Alma/Lin-

Shift Happens

Ghostly signs of my ex were everywhere: his desk was gone, but indentations remained in the carpet, holes gaped in the closets where clothes had hung and missing pieces of furniture left cavities in the rooms. We had just divorced. The year was 1998. The wrangling between us took its toll and left me with an urgent need to change the angry, moody and muddled atmosphere. I wanted my now-half-empty studio/home to feel untroubled and cheerful for myself and my animals. I wanted to reclaim my space.

However, my recovery got interrupted by another loss. My old dog, a black-and-white border collie, couldn't handle the stress of a separated family. She died of heart failure that same month. The hollowness of the house without my pup felt unbearable. I longed for her unconditional affection, her messy fur and her wet nose. I buried her in the backyard.

Shortly after that my kitty, who comforted me by sleeping on my pillow at night, had a seizure and soon died. I buried him next to the puppy. The consequences of our decision fell hard upon me.

Uncertain how to cope, I got in my own way of moving on by constantly struggling with my surroundings. Convinced I had to leave my home and find a new space kept me conflicted because my studio was my solace and I couldn't leave it behind. I was stuck, unable to move back or forward.

The turning point came when my women's group arrived one evening ready for another night of sharing, carping, bonding and wine drinking. After some talk about changing the energy in my space, from morose to carefree, we concocted a plan. We gathered pots and pans, wooden spoons, a whisk, corkscrew, a couple of spray bottles and a jar of vanilla.

We turned on every light in the twenty-five-hundred square foot space and lit it up like a beacon with light beaming through all the skylights. We went to work.

We sprayed every room and each corner with the fresh scent of vanilla and danced under the droplets. Eagerly, each of us grabbed a noisemaker and marched through the rooms banging pots, singing, laughing and shouting reclaiming the space by chasing away the demons.

It sounds silly now, but the willingness of friends to do the outrageous or inconceivable or questionable was uplifting. The experience shifted me enough that I knew I wanted to stay there for a while. The chaotic energy and bad memories were replaced with a celebration of caring friends, laughing and singing. Implausible shift happens.

Hope Is Exhausting

Unregulated toxic chemicals, urban air quality, smog and acid rain were some of the environmental issues of the 1980's. I volunteered to work on problems like those and found companies like Dow Chemical and the coal-fired power plants at odds with ecological health and well-being. Looking back. I wish I had the environmental passion now that I did in Colorado in the 80s. But did that passion really make a difference?

I worked on air quality concerns like my life depended on it, and I surely believed everyone's life did. Amid growing public anxiety, these issues of dirty air and the increased level of chemical exposure in our homes seemed to me an obvious problem while being indisputable. I believed that when everyone saw the facts, the jig would be up for the polluting, toxic-emitting industries. My job was to be out front with these troublesome facts.

I volunteered with the Colorado Environmental Coalition. The 1980's saw a growth of grassroots organizations in reaction to the election of Ronald Reagan—who set out to dismantle our safeguards. Regulations that were put in place to protect the public health soon were under the knife.

Reagan named a task force headed by George Bush that recommended changes that would reduce the so-called "burden" on industry. That executive order mandated that any regulations had to first pass an economic benefits standard thereby eliminating the health benefits. He proceeded to cut the Environmental Protection Agency staff by approximately 30 percent and their budget by 12 percent.

We had our work cut out for us. I spent time organizing, lobbying locally and in D.C., I arranged press conferences, set up town hall meetings and wrote position papers. I was fueled by my beliefs that corporations should do no harm and that the government would be responsible for making and enforcing laws to keep us safe. I couldn't conceive that both the government and industry were in bed together. Columnist Jim Hightower said, "our leaders sold us out to corporate hucksters who fed us ideological lies."

For years I believed I could make a difference, but that eventually gave way to disillusionment. Thirty-five years later most of those toxic chemicals are not regulated by the EPA. Recently the Obama administration set stricter controls on the polluting industries and endorsed the efforts of the Paris Climate Conference...soon to be dismantled.

I still feel passionate and discouraged about our environmental plight. Occasionally I add my name to an online petition, with the belief I'm reassuring some volunteer—a volunteer who has the same enthusiasm and hope that I once did to encourage the best policies for the common good.

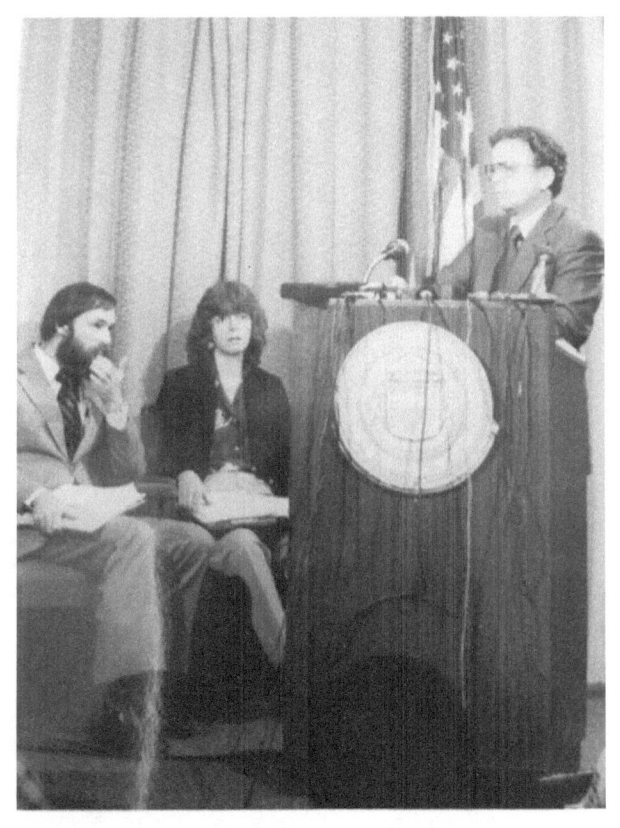

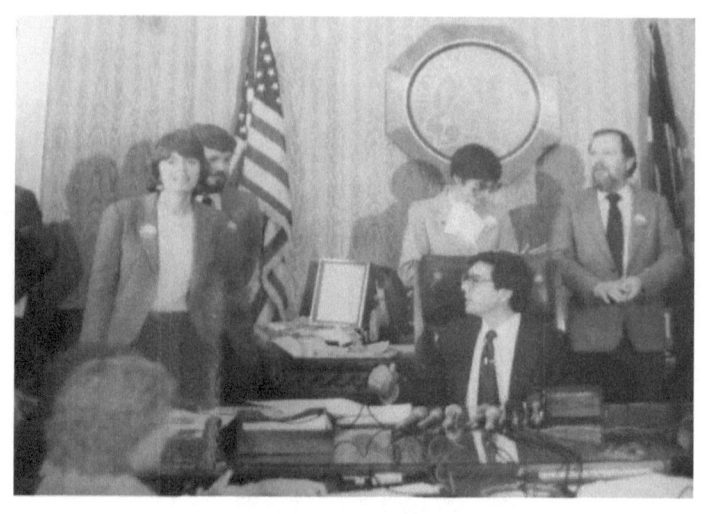

And Yet We Persist

"I am stockpiling antibiotics for the apocalypse even as I await the blossoming of paperwhites on the windowsill in the kitchen." Author Anne Lamott wrote those words referring to her anticipation or dread regarding the environment, politics, friends and family.

Often I'm less optimistic than I want to be. The political and environmental climates have me in a heated frenzy most of the time. I have temperature issues anyway. Yes, hot flashes! And some days hope springs eternal that the heat will go away. Yet, mostly I despair that I'm stuck with a blasting internal furnace.

I used to have a t-shirt (one I didn't wear) that read: *They're not hot flashes, They're POWER SURGES*. I didn't find that helpful.

Long ago I had a favorite red t-shirt that said *A woman without a man is like a fish without a bicycle*. I loved that shirt and wore it out. Those were the days when feminists were seeking to get the Equal Rights Amendment ratified. That campaign felt momentous—essential to our future. It was a call to rise up and we did, an honest power surge.

There appeared to be a lot of hope then, considering the amendment had a wide, bipartisan support until conservative opposition mobilized in panic of women being drafted and losing alimony, among other things. We're not all the same in our expectations of what we want in life, but everyone, I feel, should have equal rights to pursue them.

Twenty years ago I received an Uppity Woman Award in the Colorado Woman News. They listed my current professional accomplishments. I felt proud of that title and recognition then. Uppity felt bold and powerful. But it really means brazen and impertinent and maybe pushy and insistent. Would it have been necessary to pursue uppity if the ERA was in place? It is tempting to imagine a life without having to insist on personal power.

Yet, I haven't entirely despaired about equal rights. Today women are taking back the narrative and have initiated the #Me Too and #Times Up movement. I'm feeling a gush of energy, a blossoming of paperwhites—a power surge.

Colorado Woman News

The Voice of the Women's Community

December 1999

CW... Uppity Women

Denver artist **Karen White** has been elected president of the Women's Art Center and Gallery. White's one-woman show, "shrines, spheres and sanctuaries," recently completed a summer-long run at the Humerickhouse Museum in Ohio. She is a Year 2000 recipient of a grant from the Colorado Council on the Arts. She was additionally recognized by the Colorado Women's Leadership Coalition as one of their 1999 Women Leaders of Excellence Award for her work with the Women's Arts Center and Gallery.

In 1999, the National Endowment for the Arts and the President's Committee on the Arts and Humanities elected White to join a national jury that helped select awards for their joint Arts and Humanities Programs for Children and Youth at Risk. The awards were presented by First Lady Hillary Rodham Clinton in Washington, D.C. Oct. 26.

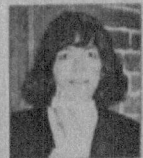

Karen White

ABOUT THE AUTHOR

One of Karen White's primary interests has been to promote the arts, including writing, in local communities. She has received public art grants for community based art. And she co-founded the *Women's Arts Center Gallery* and the *Broadway Corridor Arts Alliance* in Denver. She currently serves on the *Winter Haven Cultural Arts Advisory Committee* in Florida.

Karen has been a National Endowment for the Arts *Alternative for Youth* national juror and *The President's Committee on the Arts* national juror.

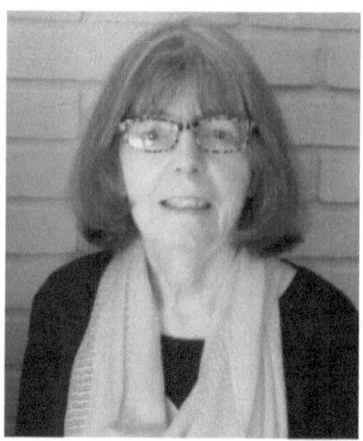

Karen is a member of several arts organizations and was voted into the prestigious *National Association of Women Artists* in New York City. She is also listed in Who's Who of American Artists and Who's Who of American Women.

Her artwork has been exhibited nationally as well as internationally and has been reviewed and published in national magazines and books. This is her first book.

www.ingramcontent.com/pod-product-compliance
Lightning Source LLC
Chambersburg PA
CBHW031423210526
45464CB00005B/2026